THE LEEDS RHINOS MISCELLANY

PHIL CAPLAN

The History Press

Acknowledgements

Thanks to Phil Daly at the Rhinos for his support of the project, and Ros, life's proof-reader.

Dedication

For JH and HJ – one an inspiration on the field, the other the finest of company off it.

First published 2010

The History Press
The Mill, Brimscombe Port
Stroud, Gloucestershire, GL5 2QG
www.thehistorypress.co.uk

British Library Cataloguing in Publication Data.
A catalogue record for this book is available from the British Library.

ISBN 978 0 7524 5218 0

Typesetting and origination by The History Press
Printed in Great Britain
Manufacturing managed by Jellyfish Print Solutions Ltd

FOREWORD

I am in an almost unique position having played for and now fortunate enough to be involved in the running of what is one of the biggest and best known club sides in world rugby.

Headingley Carnegie Stadium has always been something and somewhere special whether as a player – and it has certainly inspired the opposition on numerous occasions – or just to be able to have the resonant surroundings as a work environment.

Of course, in the modern, summer era, the club and the game have changed dramatically. Most of my meetings now take place in the vibrant, community-accessed Carnegie Café in the recently built stand of the same name, for example.

The partnership with Leeds Met Carnegie to provide such a facility illustrates just how far the sport has altered and moved forward. Leeds have always been a progressive club and their current, unprecedented success on the field is the result of a lot of hard work by a number of dedicated people in all areas, not just on the field where it is the most visible and important. We are proud to be building a legacy – it is a real kudos for the city, especially when wearing the mantle of World Champions – and we are very aware of the history at Headingley Carnegie and our place within it.

Anything that commemorates the names, deeds, records and trivia surrounding the name is to be welcomed and this captivating collection by the Rhinos Heritage Officer Phil Caplan will hopefully fascinate, delight and raise the odd eyebrow for the committed fan and curious spectator alike.

It is only by having a context of what has gone on in the past that we can make sense of the present and build for the future. My only disappointment is that my endeavours on the famous field were not sufficiently noteworthy to merit an entry! Mind you, I am one of the few players to have played in both a Leeds/Bradford derby for the Loiners, as was, and the Wigan/St Helens equivalent, when I went for one game on loan at Central Park.

Now there's a fact.

Gary Hetherington, 2010

THREE-PEAT

There could be no more appropriate time to fête the deeds of the Rhinos and reflect upon the facts, figures and trivia that surround one of the great names and venues in world sport. An unprecedented third consecutive Super League Grand Final victory in the 2009 decider confirmed this current generation's right to be regarded as the greatest Leeds team of all time, as they shattered and set a host of records at Old Trafford. Most 'greatest ever' evaluations are retrospective; a renaissance cannot be created, but there can be no doubt that the five years from 2004, which have included four championship titles – one more than the previous 114 years put together – along with two World Club Challenge victories, a brace of League Leaders' Shields, a Challenge Cup final and a further Grand Final appearance represents a sustained period of continued excellence that is unparalleled in the distinctive blue and amber. In a salary-capped sport, to take out the top prize three times running is as astonishing as it is remarkable. The only club to better the feat is the all-conquering Wigan outfits of the mid-1980s to mid-1990s but, being full-time and highly capitalised to everyone else's part-time status, theirs was not a level playing field. Excluding them for that reason, since the Northern Union, as was, was formed during the breakaway in 1895, no club has won three Championships in a row, such is the magnitude of the Rhinos' achievement. Perhaps equally as importantly for a club that has prided itself on the style with which it plays, the 2009 vintage were the leading points scorers in the competition, made the most clean breaks and had the top try-scorer who was ten ahead of his nearest rival in domestic competition. Leeds fans, who in the past had been something of apologists as followers of an underachieving, heavily resourced club with a crushing weight of expectation, experienced a genuine feeling of pride in excellence because of the calibre of the players wearing the shirt in this professional era. Ultimate victory was achieved without sacrificing inherent integrity and honesty and with the core values of genuine mateship, strength in unity, family and a respect of history to the fore.

RHINOS 2009 GRAND FINAL RECORDS

- First side to win three consecutive Grand Finals
- Kevin Sinfield first player to captain four Grand Final-winning sides
- Lee Smith first player to score tries in three consecutive Grand Finals. Even more meritoriously, they are all from different positions, wing in 2007, full-back 2008 and centre 2009
- Lee Smith shares with team-mate Danny McGuire and Bradford's Michael Withers the most career tries in Grand Finals with four, Smith in three games, McGuire four and Withers six
- Kevin Sinfield extends his records for Grand Final career goals to 18, including one drop goal, and points tally to 35 in five appearances
- Rob Burrow becomes first player to drop a goal in two Grand Finals
- Jamie Peacock becomes the first player to own enough Grand Final rings to have to use two hands to put them on, winning his sixth
- Kevin Sinfield becomes the first Leeds player to have won the Harry Sunderland Trophy for man of the match in the Championship decider (2009) and the Lance Todd Trophy for the best individual performance in a Challenge Cup final (2005)

ICON OF A GENERATION I – KEVIN SINFIELD

A virtuoso performance in the 2009 Grand Final, which saw him emphatically voted man of the match, reconfirmed that skipper Kevin Sinfield is the heartbeat of the greatest ever Leeds side. His prowess as he commanded the Old Trafford turf was summed up by three different kicks that changed the complexion of the game and further underlined a modern rugby intelligence that is almost without parallel in the British game. When his side were under the cosh in the opening quarter and St Helens looked like taking decisive hold, he pinned them back with a glorious 40/20 which changed the momentum of the contest. Having drawn level by the break, his restart to the second half found touch to not only set up immediate field position but to further sow the seeds of doubt in the increasingly fragile Saints mentality.

From the scrum that resulted, he dropped the goal that put Leeds ahead and further ratcheted up the pressure to sap the resolve of their doughty opponents. It was typical Sinfield, masterly at the right moment. Even that, though, paled by comparison to one of the tackles of any season as he tracked back from seemingly nowhere to nail Kyle Eastmond in the corner in the ultimate game-turning moment. His tackling stats are invariably astonishing, although that side of his game is often undervalued by the watching critics. In each of the three consecutive title-winning seasons he has topped the Leeds count and in 2007 and 2008 was more than 120 ahead of his nearest team-mate. What he proved again, extending his record as the finest Leeds captain in history when he picked up the Championship trophy for the fourth time in 2009, was that he is incomparable as a leader. Quietly assertive, his drive, determination, ambition and constant pursuit of excellence make him the ultimate man to follow and he has come to represent the best of the modern professional sportsman both within the dressing room and as an ambassador for the club and the code. On the pitch, when the final whistle went to signal the completion of the quest to land the Super League XIV title, the realisation that his side had become the first to win three consecutive Grand Finals began to sink in and he showed the human emotion of what that achievement meant. It was not about winning one game, but put the unstinting efforts of three years into relief. The tear in his eye said everything about the meticulous preparation, togetherness and sacrifice he and his players had put in, not just for that eighty minutes but day in, day out without fuss or deserved acclaim and recognition. With all that going through his mind, allied to the joy of winning, he then had to make a speech before collecting the trophy and joining his team-mates, live to those in the ground and the watching millions throughout the world. Measured and articulate, his last sentence dedicated the win to John Holmes, Leeds' greatest ever servant who had passed away the week before. To have the presence of mind to do that, which meant a tremendous amount to so many associated with the club, was not only further indication of his compassion but said so much about the spirit and ethos he has inculcated within the current group.

A student of history as well as a graduate in sports science, he is the epitome and essence of what it should mean to be a professional sportsman. Oldham-born, despite being only 29, he has already had a testimonial at the club he joined on scholarship as a 12-year-old and one to whom he has said he is committed for life. He was earmarked as a leader from his early days skippering successful Academy sides with his perception and composure immediately evident. In 2004 he became the first Leeds skipper to lift the title for 32 years and the following March the first to see his men crowned World Club Champions. During Super League XII, he became the first Leeds player in history – and second in Super League – to play and score in every match during a season, a total of 36 games and 306 points. That consecutive run was extended to 63 matches in all competitions, 52 of them Super League games, and was only ended when he played for England in France. In all, he posted 570 points during that time, the sequence both a club and competition record. He made his first team debut as a 16-year-old and was appointed skipper in 2003 at the age of 22. By the end of the 2009 campaign he stood second in the club's all-time points scoring list having kicked his 1,000th goal that year and passed the 2,000 points barrier – fittingly during the 2008 Grand Final – and is closing in on Lewis Jones' records in both categories which looked unsurpassable. Although a member of the squad that won the 1999 Challenge Cup, scoring two tries at Widnes in the quarter-final, he did not play at Wembley. In a competition that has seen him miss out twice since in finals, he won the Lance Todd Trophy at Cardiff in 2005 in a beaten side. He made his representative debut for England in the 2000 World Cup, scoring a hat-trick against Russia, and has won 14 Great Britain caps. Player of the Year in 2005 and again in 2009, he has been selected for the mythical Super League 'Dream Team' on four occasions and made over 300 starts for the club. Named as the 'International Loose Forward of the Year' at the 2009 Rugby League International Federation Awards, he gained further recognition worldwide when making the Golden Boot short list.

CHAMPIONSHIP VICTORIES IN A WORD

1961 – REALISATION

- Leeds finally win their first title after waiting 70 years

1969 – BRUTAL

- It's war as the Loiners summon up one last attack to beat local rivals Castleford

1972 – RETRIBUTION

- Saints win the cup but a week later a young Leeds side gain instant revenge

2004 – EXHILARATION

- After a wait of 32 years a new generation of Rhinos finally experience being top dogs

2007 – BREATHTAKING

- St Helens are ripped apart in glorious, emphatic style

2008 – DEFIANT

- Thrashed by Saints in the play-offs, the Rhinos turn the tables to down the overwhelming favourites

2009 – FULFILLMENT

- The closest-knit of groups make history with a third consecutive Grand Final win

THEY CAME TO HEADINGLEY BY CAR

A bunch of Loiners who had their own transport:

Phil Ford
John Riley
John Bentley
Oliver Morris
Fred Pickup
Mickey Vann
David Healey
Maurice Lucas
Steve Morris
Chev Walker
Ernie & Ossie Deysel

FIVE HUNDRED UP!

Centre Keith Senior passed an astonishing landmark when Leeds faced Hull at the KC Stadium in July 2009. Super League's record appearance maker and try-scorer took the field for the 500th time, the 33-year-old former Great Britain international becoming the first player in the modern era to reach the milestone. He led the side out and celebrated in suitable style, scoring the 230th try of his distinguished career in a 43–30 triumph. A member of the Sheffield side that ran out for the opening match of the summer era in Paris, scoring a try in defeat, he was part of the Eagles side that memorably and sensationally beat Wigan at Wembley in 1998 before moving to Leeds the following season, ostensibly as a replacement for Brad Godden.

Since then he has played on the biggest stages but felt the pressure of this special personal achievement. 'It was the first time I've felt a bit anxious about going into a game,' he said afterwards. 'It had been hyped up quite a bit, but it's something that I'm very proud that I've finally achieved.' Ironically, he also made his 300th appearance for Leeds against Hull, scoring twice against them at the end of May. As well as being virtually indestructible, he is the perfect winger's centre as he again illustrated in 2009 when he moved from the right – where he had formed a sensational partnership with Scott Donald – to the left, which saw Ryan Hall head the try charts thanks in part to the imperious service he received from the man on his inside. Paying tribute to his amazing appearance record, Rhinos coach Brian McClennan commented, 'To get 500 games in the professional era is a tremendous achievement and there's more to come. It's a really good effort and our whole team is really proud to be involved in such an historic occasion.'

EXPANDING HORIZONS

Since the advent of Super League, Leeds have played in five foreign countries and visited two others for pre-season training. In 2001, they made their first of three visits to Jacksonville, Florida, to prepare for the Super League campaign, winning the Sunshine State Challenge at Alltel Stadium. In a semi-final which saw Brett Mullins, Tonie Carroll and Robbie Mears make their debuts, they beat Gary Mercer's Halifax 18–10 – for whom Jamie Thackray scored a try. The Rhinos went on to dispose of Huddersfield 28–0 in the final later the same day.

The following year, the Rhinos reverted to their natural habitat when visiting South Africa but it was Widnes who sent a warning to the other Super League clubs with a 22–10 victory. The teams met at the Herman Immelman Stadium in Johannesburg in a clash screened live on local television. It was the Vikings who adjusted best to the altitude, heat and second-half downpour to secure a win in front of more than 1,000 fans.

The blue and amber travellers were back in America in 2008 when a hugely profiled game, attended by South Sydney co-owner Russell Crowe and his celebrity entourage, attracted a capacity 12,500 fans to the Hodges Stadium at the University of North Florida. Despite heavy rain, Leeds beat the Rabbitohs 26–24 in a distinct game of two halves to pick up the Australia Day Challenge Trophy. Leeds led 26–0 at the break having given their top liners a run out and held on with predominantly young squad members in the ranks in the second half; skipper Kevin Sinfield having been withdrawn from the fray at the interval to fly home for the birth of his second child.

In 2009, a young Leeds outfit this time came from behind to defeat promoted Salford 12–10 at the same venue to successfully end the Rhinos Florida Stampede. Despite trailing 10–0 early on, a side shorn of most of their star names –

Jamie Peacock having flown home early this time to witness the arrival of his daughter – posted late scores to keep their unbeaten American record going.

Overseas training camps were also staged in Lanzarote in 2004 and Dublin three years later, both as precursors to the club winning the title, but there was no match played at the end of them.

Competitively, Leeds have appeared five times in Wales, losing in two Challenge Cup finals but winning three league fixtures, twice in Scotland where again the cup was an Achilles heel but a regular season fixture not so, and seven times in France, which have all been Super League fixtures, one an 'on the road game' against London to help test the market for the arrival of Catalans Dragons in Perpignan.

Leeds Rhinos on their passport travels

USA – Pre-season, P 4 W 4
2001 – Halifax 18–10, Huddersfield 28–0
2008 – South Sydney 26–24
2009 – Salford 12–10

SOUTH AFRICA – Pre-season, P 1 L 1
2002 – Widnes 10–22

SCOTLAND – P 2 W 1 L 1
2000 – Challenge Cup final – Bradford 18–24
2009 – Murrayfield Magic – Catalans 36–16

WALES – P 5 W 3 L 2
2003 – Challenge Cup final – Bradford 20–22
2005 – Challenge Cup final – Hull 24–25
2007 – Millennium Magic – Bradford 42–38
2008 – Millennium Magic – Bradford 40–26
2009 – Super League – Celtic Crusaders 68–0

FRANCE – Super League, P7 W 4 L 3

1996 – Paris St Germain 40–14
1997 – Paris St Germain 28–18
2005 – London Broncos 24–32 (in Perpignan)
2006 – Catalans 58–10
2007 – Catalans 22–30
2008 – Catalans 37–24
2009 – Catalans 30–32

Total record with suitcase in tow – P 19 W 12 L 7

SO GOOD TO BE BACK HOME

Although the average attendance at Headingley Carnegie watching the Rhinos in 2009 dropped slightly – in part due to a combination of the recession, having two less well supported sides new to the competition and a reduction in the number of travelling fans – a notable landmark was achieved as the two and a half millionth paying customer passed through the electronic turnstiles since the switch to summer in 1996. Allowing for the fact that the opening season was a fallow one with uncertainties over the viability of the side on the field and club off it, that represents an astonishing fanbase that allowed the Rhinos to be regarded as the best supported of either code in the oval ball game in the later years of the noughties. The biggest number of fans to attend was in 2005 when not far short of half a million ventured into Leeds 6 on match night, with the highest average two seasons later when there was one less home match on the calendar. The number of season ticket holders is currently greater than the average attendance in 1996 and the overall increase from the Super League I to XIV has been 85 per cent. In 2007, a crowd of

19,226 for the mid-September clash with Wakefield Wildcats saw the Rhinos post their highest average attendance since the Second World War.

Year	Home Games	Ave. Attendance	Total
1996	11	8,581	94,391
1997	11	11,005	121,055
1998	11	12,150	133,650
1999	15	13,465	201,975
2000	14	12,635	176,890
2001	14	12,907	180,698
2002	14	12,197	170,758
2003	14	12,849	179,886
2004	14	16,028	224,392
2005	14	17,011	238,154
2006	14	14,125	197,750
2007	13	17,516	227,708
2008	13	17,043	221,559
2009	13	15,774	205,062
TOTAL	185	13,806	2,573,928

THEY PLAYED HERE TWICE

Historically, Leeds had a reputation for never re-signing players, no matter how many realised what they were missing once it was too late. The greatest exception to that unwritten rule was Kiwi Gary Mercer, an all-action desperado who began as a rampaging winger, moved to centre and ended up as one of the hardest-working back-rowers in the sport. He initially came to Headingley under Doug Laughton's stewardship in August 1992 and then returned to answer a call for help at the end of the 2001 season, as injuries mounted.

During his first spell at the club he appeared in Challenge Cup finals in 1994 and 1995 and two years later, under compatriot Dean Bell, was appointed skipper. In six and a half seasons at the club he made 164 appearances scoring 43 tries, his longest spell in the British game after initially coming over to play for Bradford and having stints with Halifax, Warrington and Castleford. He made his second debut at Castleford on Saturday 18 August 2001 after returning from Warrington, the club from which he had initially joined Leeds. In the international arena, he represented New Zealand on 21 occasions, scoring four tries, including touring three times.

Dean Bell also played for Leeds in two different guises, although they could not have been more of a contrast. As a youngster, fresh from touring with the Maoris and a season at fledgling Carlisle, he moved to Headingley for the 1983/4 campaign, scoring a try on his debut – a memorable home defeat of then Champions Hull K.R. in the second round of the John Player Cup – and went on to pick up a winners' medal in that competition. He was set to return the following season after a spell at Eastern Suburbs but elected to follow his mentor Graham Lowe to Wigan instead, with Leeds' blessing. In 1995, having become an integral part of Wigan's exceptional trophy-winning side and led Auckland into the NRL, he returned to Headingley supposedly as an assistant to head coach Doug Laughton. He inherited the job when Laughton left unexpectedly and, in his second season, the first of Super League which saw the club in desperate shape off the field, he was forced to don the boots in an effort to stave off the distinct possibility of relegation. In a home match, billed as a 'four-pointer' against fellow strugglers Paris St Germain, he made a one-off return, scoring a vital try to secure a crucial win.

THEY SAID IT

'I'm hoping to look up a few of my old mates when we play at Leeds. I'd particularly like to see John Holmes, I think I helped make him look a good player!'

Tongue-in-cheek comment from then London Broncos coach Tony Currie on his return to Headingley

PLAYER-COACHES

Leeds have only had two player-coaches – one by default – although Daryl Powell retired his boots in 2000 to take up the reins. Syd Hynes had a golden six-year spell in charge between 1975 and 1981, winning a trophy every season and never tasting defeat in seven finals as the supremo. For the first two seasons, the capture from Leeds NALGO RU balanced the roles, twice winning Yorkshire Cup medals at scrum-half and then back in his more normal centre's berth. Rugged and uncompromising, during the 1976/7 season he gradually swapped tracksuit for one of Burton's finest, coaxing the side to a stunning Wembley triumph against hot favourites Widnes before announcing the end of a 13-year, fiercely competitive playing career. He had made over 350 appearances in blue and amber which yielded 158 tries and 188 goals. The player-coach by necessity rather than design was one-match Dean Bell, who earlier in his star-studded Wigan career had been surprised on the field at Central Park (after the cherry and whites had customarily beaten Leeds) by Eamonn Andrews and his big, red *This is Your Life* book to the tumultuous acclaim of both sets of fans who had been asked to stay behind. When he took on the role of Director of Youth Development, he presided over one of the best crop of juniors in the club's history, leading them to consecutive Academy Championship successes and instilling his supreme winning edge.

1996 – ANNUS HORRIBILIS

The start of the ill-fated 1996 season found Leeds desperately unprepared for the move to summer and start of Super League I. That was illustrated when, encompassing the first three matches of the campaign, a top line player left each week while the Challenge Cup was in progress, prior to the start of the regular season. Before travelling to Second Division – effectively third tier – Swinton in the opening round, a failure to present James Lowes with a new contract saw the hooker join rivals Bradford without receiving a fee for one of the code's brightest prospects. There he became one of the best and most consistent rakes of the modern era, bowing out with a try-scoring triumph in the 2003 Grand Final with the Bulls.

Another of the Hunslet area's finest ever products, Garry Schofield, made his final appearance of 251 in blue and amber in that scrappy and fortunate 27–22 win at Gigg Lane. He tore a pectoral muscle and, by the time it had recovered, he had agreed to move to First Division Huddersfield. For the following round Leeds drew Warrington at Wilderspool and, with the ranks in obvious increasing disarray, were expected to capitulate. They put in arguably their best performance of the year to register a heartening 30–10 success, a match in which former All Black stellar centre Craig Innes scored a try on what was to prove to be his last match in a Leeds shirt. The departure of 'Postie' to crack Australian outfit Manly – or the Silvertails as they were somewhat disparagingly known and frequently likened to Leeds with their accumulation of talent without a commensurate accrual of silverware – was an acrimonious one. The Australian game was riven between Rupert Murdoch's planned Super League and the Kerry Packer-backed ARL and with the increasingly likely advent of two competitions as a result, there was a desperate scramble for players. Innes agreed to join the Sea Eagles who remained in the ARL competition, Leeds initially seeking an injunction to stop him playing for the rival governing body, the RFL here having agreed to become the European arm of Super League. He left regardless, Leeds then deciding to pursue a fee of £200,000, again backed by the RFL but ultimately to no avail. The strong running three-quarter subsequently went on to win a Grand Final with Manly in 1997, under the tutelage of former Leeds coach Malcolm Reilly.

In the quarter-final of the cup, Leeds won 35–24 at Halifax but again at a cost, Kiwi international Tony Kemp – effectively Schofield's replacement – breaking his arm. With such a run of ill luck and bad judgement, it was hardly surprising that the club spent most of the rest of the season fighting against relegation.

GOLDEN BOYS

Luke Burgess became the 68th Leeds player to win either a Championship medal or Grand Final ring when he stepped up to receive his prized possession at Old Trafford in 2009. Eight of his team-mates were picking up their fourth, a club record, six of them having come through the academy ranks and one, Kiwi Ali Lauitiiti, from overseas. Father and son David and Danny Ward have the distinction of being the sole decorated family, 32 years apart. All three of Ian Kirke's rings have come from the bench as did David Hick's two medals.

Leeds players who have won the Championship

Four times – (2004, 2007, 2008, 2009)
Keith Senior, Kevin Sinfield, Danny McGuire, Matt Diskin, Ryan Bailey, Ali Lauitiiti, Rob Burrow, Jamie Jones-Buchanan (total 8)

Three times – (2007, 2008, 2009)
Scott Donald, Lee Smith, Kylie Leuluai, Jamie Peacock, Carl Ablett, Ian Kirke (total 6)

Twice – John Atkinson (1969, 1972), Ray Batten (1969, 1972), John Langley (1969, 1972), David Hick (1969, 1972), Brent Webb (2007, 2009), Gareth Ellis (2007, 2008), Ryan Hall (2008, 2009) (total 7)

Once
1961 – Ken Thornett, Wilf Rosenberg, Derek Hallas, Vince Hattee, Eddie Ratcliffe, Lewis Jones, Colin Evans, Don Robinson, Barry Simms, Trevor Whitehead, Jack Fairbank, Dennis Goodwin, Brian Shaw
1969 – Bev Risman, Ronnie Cowan, Syd Hynes, Bernard Watson, Mick Shoebottom, Barry Seabourne, Mick Clark, Tony Crosby, Ken Eyre, Mick Joyce, Bill Ramsey
1972 – John Holmes, Alan Smith, Les Dyl, Alan Hardisty, David Barham, Terry Clawson, David Ward, Tony Fisher, Bob Haigh, Phil Cookson, Fred Pickup
2004 – Richard Mathers, Mark Calderwood, Chev Walker, Marcus Bai, Danny Ward, Chris McKenna, David Furner, Barrie McDermott, Willie Poching
2007 – Clinton Toopi
2008 – Nick Scruton
2009 – Luke Burgess (total – 47)

SELECT BAND

Twenty-one Leeds players have both a Championship medal or Grand Final ring and Wembley Challenge Cup winners' medal in their collection. Lewis Jones and Don Robinson were the first, the only remaining members of the 1957 Twin Towers victory over Barrow who ran out at Odsal as the Championship grail was finally captured four years later.

Championship and Cup glory
The following players are the most select of bands, having winner's medals in both of the most prestigious competitions in blue and amber:

Lewis Jones, Don Robinson, Bev Risman, Alan Smith, Syd Hynes, Bernard Watson, John Atkinson, Mick Shoebottom, Barry Seabourne, Mick Clark, Tony Crosby, Ken Eyre, Bill Ramsey, Ray Batten, John Langley, Mick Joyce, Les Dyl, John Holmes, David Ward, Phil Cookson, Barrie McDermott (total – 21)

ICON OF A GENERATION 2 – JOHN HOLMES

It is a mark of the esteem with which John Holmes was held that, at barely a few days' notice after his passing at the tragically young age of 57 in late September 2009, over 100 ex-players gathered on the pitch in silent tribute to him before the Super League play-off against Catalans Dragons. It was not only former Loiners who showed publicly how much the maestro meant but international colleagues and administrators joined the heartfelt homage to the Leonardo da Vinci of Leeds rugby – a true artist among the artisans. A product of the 1960s, his talents were comparable to those of George Best, honing his skill and ability to look after himself on a school playground with his elder brothers, which left him able to pass, kick and, perhaps most importantly, bring the best out of those around him. He became the ultimate local (although reluctant) hero, the most durable and arguably best ever to don the colours he so cherished. He was one whose skills delighted, whose presence was eagerly awaited each week, who thrilled and conjured magical moments and had an enviable talent that was seemingly effortless and timeless – a genuine match definer.

Every generation has its signature player and for Leeds fans, attuned to almost continual success in the second great era of the club in the late 1960s and throughout the 1970s, that was John Holmes; the unassuming Kirkstall boy who walked to and from the ground where his heroes played and became a Loiners legend. If Headingley has a tradition for the manner in which the game should be played and the virtues that would see it won, then he was the very essence of what that stood for; grace, style, sportsmanship, *savoir faire*, modesty – he combined them all in a glorious career that spanned four decades. However you define greatness, John Holmes – for whom the term 'mercurial' in a rugby sense was coined – fulfilled every criterion. For those who saw him – and there were masses considering he played for Leeds for an astonishing, double testimonial 21 seasons – watching him cajole, toy and orchestrate his side was an absolute joy. A majestic ball-handler, able to unlock any defence, he was a superb cover tackler as he showed in his early days as a young custodian, had pace and a supreme rugby intelligence. Not that such influence was planned, his genius was instinctive. Memories are made of silky interventions, sublime performances, the setting up of game changing tries, they cannot be purely about statistics but the list of his achievements gives him the right to be ranked among the all-time greats, not only in blue and amber, but across the code.

A master in 19 finals, and architect of victory in the majority of them, he served notice of his talent with 23 points, from a try and ten goals, on his debut as a 16-year-old in a Lazenby Cup match against Hunslet in 1968, just after signing on. A regular at full-back when Bev Risman retired, scoring a hat-trick in a Yorkshire Cup final with his imperious linking in 1972, he was equally effective at centre for county and country before becoming one of the most gifted stand-offs in the sport. His one-handed, lobbed pass over 30 metres to send John Atkinson racing in for the decisive try in the 1973 John Player final went in to folklore. Often the victim of horrendously timed late challenges as opponents' frustrations sought the only route left to them to try to undermine his ability, he was also one of the bravest around as he showed when taking the Loiners to Wembley in 1978; the key to defeating Featherstone in the semi-final with a glorious try despite a gaping leg wound. Internationally, he played in two World Cup finals for Great Britain, a winner in 1972 and loser Down Under five years later. His 10 goals and 26 points against New Zealand in Pau in the first of them were both records. His final Test appearance, against the 1982 Kangaroo 'Invincibles' at Central Park, came eleven years after his debut when he had played at centre against the Kiwis at Headingley, scoring two goals and two drop goals. Had he elected to continue kicking, there is every likelihood that he would have topped Lewis Jones' records at Leeds. In his second full season he slotted 159 goals, only seven behind the Welsh wizard, but instead he chose to wow his army of devoted followers with his glorious timing, sidestep, outstanding tactical kicking and passing ability. By the time he retired – having been tempted onto the bench for one final first-team appearance at the start of the 1989 season – he had pulled on the Leeds shirt a record 625 times, 82 more than his nearest challenger. Like the goal-kicking duties, which he felt inhibited his natural flair despite being so good at it, so it was with the captaincy which he held for a while before deciding it affected his main role for the side. Loved by his fellow players, cherished by the home fans and admired by opposing ones, he was denied a rightful honour in arguably his finest hour when Leeds staged the then greatest comeback in Challenge Cup final history as he masterminded their jailbreak 14–12 win over St Helens in 1978, after being 10 points down. A typical, beautifully judged pass to set Mick Crane in motion started the revival in the first half and a similar one allowed Neil Hague to put David Smith over at the start of the second half. With Saints hanging on and the Lance Todd Trophy votes in – and for George Nicholls – he produced another wondrous display of dexterity, his inside ball sending Phil Cookson across, before his *coup de grâce*, a left-footed drop goal as he was falling backwards to put the Loiners ahead for the first time to set up the most dramatic of wins. As he later recalled, 'The drop goal is one of my finest memories. I've watched it since and, to be honest, I still don't know how it went over; I just knew I had to have a go. I used to practice with my wrong foot on the training pitch for a laugh just to see if I could do it and that day; bang, over it goes, unbelievable. Winning the cup with your mates was brilliant, far more important than whether or not I should have won the Lance Todd although, to be fair, all the press came in to the dressing after the match and apologised. But that was by the by, it didn't matter; we'd won the match, no problem.' He played in his last final in 1984 in the John Player Trophy making and scoring the tries that brought Leeds victory over Widnes before taking a temporary sabbatical as he toured Australia.

On his return he was persuaded to don the boots again, making occasional appearances in the first team, including masterminding an astonishing, rare victory at Knowsley Road in 1988, while player-coaching the Alliance side from back row as he selflessly passed on his craftsman's tools to the next generation. Comparisons are always drawn between the greats of yesteryear and whether they would have coped with the demands of Super League. In John Holmes' case, the modern game would have been made for him with the sport crying out for inventive, genuinely creative players who can unlock the tightest of defensive systems. He would have loved the 40/20 kick and to have had the greater protection afforded by a full-time pack, having had to develop the art of passing and leaving an arm raised to look after himself in his later years. A printer by trade, he was diagnosed with cancer which returned in particularly virulent fashion but, again, he fought that battle in his own inimitable way, out of the spotlight. He hated fuss and adoration and left life as he did the game, without ceremony. 'I've been called a reluctant hero,' he said, 'I never really did a lot of interviews in my time – although things were different then and players tended not to make the headlines or be asked as much about the game. Most often after the match it was get a wash, through the gates and go get some dinner at your mam's. If people still mention my name after so long, then that's a thrill.' With his passing, the world of Rugby League lost a rare artist, a gentleman, a crowd-pleaser and one of its most humble, loyal servants – a true hero.

TOP FIVE NICKNAMES

John 'Dinny' Campbell

Joe 'Chimpy' Busch

Frank 'Bucket' Young

Arthur 'Ginger' Thomas

Les 'Juicy' Adams

SHIRT SPONSORS

In an effort to boost the profile of their Kestrel Lager brand, brewers McEwan-Younger became the first shirt sponsors of the club. In 1981/2 they supplied various man of the match and player of the month awards but the following year their Kestrel logo was the first to be seen on a Leeds shirt other than the manufacturers, which at the time was Bukta. In 1983/4 after initially having the Youngers name on the back above the playing number, it was splashed across the front of the broad amber band, on a white background, to effectively become the first Leeds shirt sponsor. That remained the marque for five seasons, until brewing rivals Bass took over, renaming the famous stadium Bass Headingley for a short period and putting their revamped Carling Black Label motif on the jersey. When Leeds returned to Wembley in 1994 after a 16-year absence, they signed a massive £2.3 million, 10-year deal with city-based brewing giant Carlsberg-Tetley which saw the pint most synonymous with Leeds plastered across the front of the shirt, much to the delight of the fans as it brought together two of their passions. At the same time, the ground reverted back to being known just as Headingley. In 2007, the fourth name on the famous colours was the first not to be that of an alcohol manufacturer as legislation changed. Leeds Building Society took on the mantle as the club entered a period of unprecedented success. In 2006, when Catalans entered Super League and drink advertising was already banned on the continent, Leeds played in a specially adapted shirt with 'Thirsty' on the front, replacing 'Tetleys' but in the same style and design. The season before, the Rhinos had also played in Perpignan, against London in an 'on the road' fixture for the Broncos, this time changing the logo to that of Leeds Met Carnegie for a one-off.

THEY SAID IT

'I think my own club should merge, with Halifax or Leeds the obvious candidates, what a power that would create. We have worked really hard, but we look over our shoulders and see nothing happening.'

Bradford Bulls then Chairman Chris Caisley may have spoken too soon

WIGAN SHOW LITTLE CHARITY

Leeds have only been invited to appear in the Charity Shield on one occasion, having not qualified for the pre-season showcase by right, and then it turned out to be something of a poisoned chalice – although it did enable the club to break new ground. Having already been pasted twice by the last remnants of the all-conquering Wigan side of the era, first at Wembley and then, humiliatingly, in the Old Trafford Premiership final, the Loiners were asked to open the 1995/6 season – the last before the cataclysmic shift to summer and Super League – by facing the Riversiders again, in Dublin. Contested on only nine occasions and in five locations, the Charity Shield was supposed to be the league champions against the cup winners. With Wigan's dominance seeing them regularly do that double, those who they had defeated were given the opportunity to compete. Leeds also finished runners-up in the league the previous season and took part in the last ever such fixture at the Royal Dublin Showground on 13 August 1995, the venue selected because of the apparent growing interest in the code in the Emerald Isle. The arena seemed slightly incongruous, fans arriving the day before shocked to see it on the local television staging the Horse of the Year Show which undoubtedly affected the pitch, although not, maybe, in terms of a ready supply of natural nutrients for the grass. Also, as has been so often the case with Rugby League, the date clashed with the All Ireland Gaelic Football semi-final which dominated the television schedules. The crowd of just over 5,000 which did turn up – including such local luminaries as rugby union star Tony Ward who covered the match for the local press and wrote a highly complimentary report – witnessed another record-breaking performance by the cherry and whites. Their 45–20 success was a new landmark as were the 8 goals and 20 points garnered by man of the match Andy Farrell as his side carried off the Waterford Crystal Bowl. Leeds – under the new management of Hugh McGahan as they awaited coach Dean Bell, Doug Laughton having relinquished the coaching reins – were not helped by the early dismissal of Marcus Vassilakopoulos. He was despatched by referee Russell Smith in the 9th minute for allegedly tripping Nigel Wright as he went over for the first try. Tony Kemp scored on his debut for Leeds, Esene Faimalo and Mike Forshaw claiming the other touchdowns with Paul Cook kicking four goals.

FROM PLAYER'S No. 6 TO REGAL

In the 25 years of the various incarnations of the mid-season trophy that carried the John Player sponsorship brand, Leeds appeared in a fifth of the finals, winning the silverware twice. The highs came eleven years apart and, among the quarter-century of knockout competition, there were also some desperate lows, not least losing twice to Second Division opposition. In their first season in the Rugby League in 1980, Fulham claimed their biggest scalp when memorably defeating the Loiners 9–3 in the capital in front of a crowd of over 12,500, David Eckersley their hero with a try and two drop goals. There was even greater ignominy five years later when Andy Whittle's try saw lowly Barrow triumph 5–2 at Craven Park in the nadir of Peter Fox's reign in charge. In the first round in 1977/8, Leeds seemed to be cruising in a televised clash with Wigan at Headingley, leading 20–10 with barely a quarter of an hour remaining. Jimmy Nulty claimed a try and then South African winger Green Vigo his second – scorching away from a despairing John Atkinson – Nulty goaling both to level. Kevin Dick and Nulty exchanged penalties and, with a replay looming, Vigo – in his finest hour – repeated his glory dash to steal the tie in the final minute. It was such a dispiriting defeat that Atkinson temporarily retired, returning three months later to score crucial tries on the road to and at Wembley as Leeds retained the Challenge Cup. Instituted in 1971, the Player's No. 6 Trophy, as was, saw Leeds feature in drawn ties in the first two seasons. Forced into a replay at Central Park after Wigan's Colin Tyrer had landed a penalty from near half way with the final kick, Leeds heroically won the replay 12–5 despite having veteran forward Fred Pickup sent off. The following campaign, on their way to winning the trophy, Leeds thrashed Hull at home, with Syd Hynes claiming 20 points, after drawing at the Boulevard again thanks to a dramatic, last-gasp intervention, this time from Clive Sullivan who picked up a loose ball on his own line and went the length of the field. Loiners seemed to be heading for a draw the following year, at Rochdale in the third round, with the scores locked at 5–5, Bill Holliday kicking a long-range drop goal out of the mud in injury time to knockout the holders. In their 1972/3 success over Salford, scrum-half Keith Hepworth picked up the £25 man of the match award while Australian back-rower Mark Laurie put in a virtuoso display to take the individual honour in the 1983/4 John Player Special decider, against Widnes. Six of the cup finals were played at Headingley, with two records being set. A crowd high of 25,245 saw Hull beat Hull K.R. in 1981/2, the two sides surpassing that figure three years later when 79 more people saw them do battle again at Boothferry Park. In 1993/4, Castleford produced one of the great cup upsets when they set a new highest margin, defeating the great Wigan side of the era 33–2. The competition was dropped with the advent of Super League.

Leeds in the John Player Cup

1971/2 – semi-final – lost to Halifax at home 15–9
1972/3 – winners – beat Salford 12–7 in the final at Huddersfield
1973/4 – 3rd round – lost to Rochdale away 7–5
1974/5 – 3rd round – lost to Bradford away 17–7
1975/6 – 2nd round replay – lost to Hull at home 23–11
1976/7 – 3rd round – lost to Castleford at home 20–14
1977/8 – 1st round – lost to Wigan at home 25–22
1978/9 – 1st round – lost to St Helens away 16–11
1979/80 – 2nd round – lost to Leigh at home 14–7
1980/1 – 1st round – lost to Fulham away 9–3
1981/2 – 3rd round – lost to Oldham away 14–5
1982/3 – runners up – lost to Wigan 15–4 in the final at Elland Road
1983/4 – winners – beat Widnes 18–10 in the final at Wigan
1984/5 – semi-final – lost to Hull 18–6 at Boothferry Park
1985/6 – 1st round – lost to Barrow away 5–2
1986/7 – 1st round – lost to Wigan away 32–10
1987/8 – runners up – lost to St Helens 15–14 in the final at Wigan
1988/9 – 1st round – lost to Castleford at home 21–12
1989/90 – 3rd round replay – lost to Wigan away 8–0
1990/1 – 2nd round – lost to Widnes away 22–6
1991/2 – runners up – lost to Widnes 24–0 in the final at Wigan
1992/3 – 1st round – lost to St Helens away 15–14
1993/4 – 2nd round – lost to Salford away 21–12
1994/5 – 4th round – lost to Castleford at home 34–14
1995/6 – semi-final – lost to Wigan away 38–18

SEVENTH HEAVEN

The instigation of the Carnegie Floodlit 9s in 2008 drew recollections of halcyon days when the campaign traditionally ended with the W.D. and H.O. Wills Headingley Sevens, invariably televised on the BBC and which ran from 1965 to 1978. Similarly, the new season around that time opened with the Wigan 7s at Central Park. Leeds only ever won their home tournament once, in 1973, beating St Helens 21–18 in the final although for the following two years they were successful in the Wigan version. Salford had the most success in the Headingley 7s, winning four times in all, including an unprecedented hat-trick between 1968 and 1970, beating the hosts 18–14 in the third of those deciders. Leeds lost twice more in finals, against Bradford (13–10 in 1966) and Huddersfield (11–5 the following year).

Winners of the Headingley 7s

Salford – 4 times (1968, 1969, 1970, 1974)
Bradford – twice (1964, 1966)
St Helens – once (1965)
Huddersfield – once (1967)
Wakefield – once (1971)
Halifax – once (1972)
Leeds – once (1973)
Wigan – once (1975)
Castleford – once (1976)
Widnes – once (1978)
The tournament did not run in 1977

In the modern 9s incarnation, a young Leeds side has lost twice to the eventual winners, both of whom selected more experienced squads.

2008 – Lost to Huddersfield, 1st round, 32–4
2009 – Lost to Hull, final, 16–11

There was some consolation for defeat in the decider in 2009 when Academy winger Jamel Chisholm won the title of 'Rugby League's Fastest Man' after he finished ahead of Warrington's Kevin Penny and Tom Lineham of York in a sprint challenge. In taking the £1,000 prize, he covered the 96-metre course in full kit and carrying a ball in 11.1 seconds.

The BBC 2 Floodlit Trophy ran from the mid-1960s to the 1979/80 season, Leeds winning only three out of their first nine ties until 1970/1 when they won the trophy for the sole time, beating St Helens 9–5 in the final at Headingley. Castleford proved to be their nemesis in the competition, Leeds winning only one of seven encounters between the local rivals, their first two contests being drawn.

RUGBY LEAGUE HISTORY AT HEADINGLEY

1890 – Leeds v Manningham – The new Leeds club, playing in terracotta and green, won their inaugural home match at their sumptuous new headquarters, with forward George Naylor scoring the first try on the ground.

1891 – Pontefract v Wakefield – The first final played at the ground saw the sides draw the Yorkshire Cup decider 3–3 in front of a crowd of nearly 18,000.

1893 – England v Scotland – The Auld Enemy defeated England 8–0 to win the Calcutta Cup in the first international played at the venue, two years before the great split, with almost 30,000 present, the biggest attendance at a rugby match.

1895 – Leeds v Brighouse – Bob Walton's try, the only score of the match, ensured that the Loiners won their first home Northern Union fixture after the breakaway.

1897 – Batley v St Helens – Almost 14,000 fans watched the initial NU Challenge Cup final as the great Gallant Youths side of the era won 10–3.

1907 – Leeds v 'All Golds' – Former All Black George Smith led the first-ever tourists to an 8–2 victory, with the great Dally Messenger kicking a goal for the visitors.

1908 – Northern Union v 'All Golds' – Halifax forward A. Robinson scored two tries as the hosts took the inaugural Test match, 14–6, but the tourists went on to win the series.

1909 – Leeds v Australia – The first Kangaroos won a thrilling match 14–10 in front of a big Christmas Day crowd, centre Jim Devereux crossing for two tries for the tourists.

1913 – Leeds v Coventry – Every Leeds player scored in the final match of the season as the Loiners posted a club record 102–0 win, prop Fred Webster leading the way with a landmark haul of eight touchdowns.

1921 – England v Australia – Leeds' Squire Stockwell scored the decisive try as the Test series opener, and one of the most revered international encounters, was won 6–5 in front of 32,000 fans.

1932 – Leeds v Halifax – The Good Friday game was abandoned after ten minutes when a fire broke out in the North Stand, gutting it; fortunately there were no casualties.

1934 – Leeds v France – Stan Smith scored four tries as Leeds defeated Jean Galia's inaugural French tourists 25–17, 'les Tricolores' initially training at Headingley under the watchful eye of Joe Thompson.

1938 – Leeds v Swinton – Eric Harris scored the most important try in the club's history to date, his long-range interception setting up the record-breaking 'All Leeds' Championship final that gripped the city.

1938 – Leeds v Salford – In the only match ever to be played on the cricket ground because the rugby ground was frosted over, Australian Test star Vic Hey scored the sole try as Leeds won the Christmas Eve clash 5–0.

1943 – Northern Command RL v RU – Leeds back-rower Ken Jubb scored a brace of tries as League beat Union at their own game in aid of the war effort and morale.

1947 – Leeds v Bradford – Barely a fortnight after their meeting at Wembley, a record attendance of 40,175 crammed into Headingley, generating receipts of £3,297, to watch the sides draw 2–2 in a league match.

1948 – GB v Australia – Post-war Test rugby returned to these shores, as the first Great Britain side won an epic encounter 23–21 in front of over 26,500 fans.

1956 – Leeds v Australia – Only the third and last win over the tourists who were led by ex-Leeds favourite, hooker Ken Kearney, with the Green and Golds downed 18–13.

1959 – GB v Australia – The hosts levelled the series, the last they were to win at home, with a magnificent 11–10 success, Leeds hero Don Robinson was among the try-scorers.

1966 – Yorkshire v Lancashire – The ground welcomed its first floodlit match, although the Red Rose county spoiled the switch-on, winning 22–17.

1970 – GB v Australia – The World Cup final, won 12–7 by the Aussies, witnessed the notorious 'Battle of Leeds' with Billy Smith and Syd Hynes sent off; Loiner John Atkinson scoring Britain's only try.

1982 – Hull v Hull K.R. – A record-breaking crowd for the John Player Trophy of over 25,000 saw Ronnie Wileman's touchdown give the black and whites a 12–4 win over the Robins in the final.

1982 – GB v Australia – David Topliss captained his country and Steve Evans scored the only home try of the series, as the history-making 'Invincibles' swept through their tour unbeaten.

1996 – Leeds v Warrington – Super League came to Headingley, Kevin Iro scoring Leeds' first summer try but teenager Iestyn Harris stole the show with a brace as the Wolves won 22–18.

1997 – Leeds v Adelaide – The Rhinos fully embraced the concept of summer rugby as the Rams were beaten in the World Club Championship. Paul Sterling's length-of-the-field stunner still ranks as one of the best-ever tries seen on the ground.

2000 – England v Ireland – A full-blooded World Cup quarter-final saw England emerge victorious 26–16, Leeds teenager Chev Walker scoring the winning touchdown.

2006 – Leeds v Warrington – The Rhinos ran up a half-century of points, led by hat-trick hero Keith Senior, to celebrate the opening of the Carnegie Stand, the first new development at the ground for over 70 years.

2009 – Leeds v Catalans – Leeds chose to play the Dragons in the first ever 'club call', victory setting up an unprecedented fifth Grand Final in six years for the Rhinos and matching the club record of reaching a third consecutive Championship decider, last done in 1929–31.

RUGBY'S MOST UNIQUE VENUE

The world's only dual Test arena, Headingley Carnegie Stadium holds a unique place in the pantheon of worldwide sporting venues and, especially for Australians, has proved to be a terrific draw card. With legendary cricket deeds on one side of the North Stand and their rugby equivalent on the other, no other ground can boast adjacent top-class facilities in two top-ranked sports. In its time, it also hosted tennis, cycling, athletics and bowls. Originally Lot 17a of the Cardigan estate, the 22 acres of land was purchased by a group of leading entrepreneurs, politicians and sports-minded citizens, with their Chairman Lord Hawke the figurehead. They formed the Leeds Cricket, Football and Athletic Company in 1888 in order to bring top-class sport to the city. After £30,300 of work to level the ground and build the stands – including the first double-fronted one on the north side – and pavilions, the 20,000 capacity stadium opened for its inaugural rugby match just after the start of the 1890 season. It quickly became one of the most prestigious locations for sport in the country under the auspices of aiming to, 'continually improve amenities and accommodation and to provide entertainment of the highest class for all true lovers of sport.'

Under the visionary Chairmanship of Sir Edwin Airey who took the reins in 1923, major redevelopments took place, initially with the provision of extra terracing to hold 4,000 more fans. The new South Stand was completed and part-roofed in 1931, with some of the work being carried out by club players, while the old wooden North Stand was burned down ten minutes into a match against Halifax on Good Friday, 25 March 1931. Precipitously there were no casualties and by the end of the following season, a new seating and paddock facility with press areas had been completed. The record attendance at Headingley was set over Easter in 1947 when Leeds and Bradford renewed their cup final rivalry, 40,175 cramming in for the drawn derby. A second fire in August 1958 destroyed the clock tower. But that year the South Stand was fully covered. Undersoil heating was installed in 1963 and floodlights costing £14,000 three years later, subsequently updated in 1998, while an iconic spiral staircase was added to the South Stand to enable television commentators to reach the gantry. A Rugby League first electronic scoreboard followed on the Western Terrace in March 1981 to supercede the manual box at the other end. New changing rooms were unveiled in 1991 in the middle of the main stand, ending the clatter of studs on concrete from the old pavilion at the top corner adjoining the Eastern Terrace. The Paddock areas at the front of the North Stand were seated and the pavilion was turned into a series of modern banqueting suites on four floors. In 2001, capacity was slightly increased by extending the terracing around the corner in between the Western Terraces and the North Stand while the South Stand underwent a £750,000 face lift. A state of the art classroom was added on the site of the old police lookout and, in late 2005, the first major construction took place for over 70 years with the building of the three-storey, cantilever Carnegie Stand, behind the posts at the Eastern End. In a literally groundbreaking initiative, the construction – which was both seating and terrace – included a community café and twelve class and lecture rooms for partners Leeds Met Carnegie University. It also contained modern corporate boxes and function suites, including one named after Lewis Jones, to replace the permanent portakabins at the back of the old crumbling terrace. The stand, complete with bespoke Berry's clock, had a capacity of 4,550 including 1,844 seats, and was opened on 1 September 2006 by the Minister for Sport, Richard Caborn. That took the total capacity up to around 22,500 and the moment was commemorated by the release of 1,890 blue and amber balloons in recognition of the date the stadium first opened. For the 2008 Super League Final Eliminator against Wigan, the lower part of the South Stand was closed for safety reasons and the capacity reduced by 2,000 to 6,000 owing to a degeneration of the concrete terraces, partly owing to long-term water seepage. Those repairs have been given a safety certificate for two years and the club is currently drawing up plans and arranging funding for the popular side's replacement. A refurbishment of the Taverners, opened for Christmas 2008, has seen the beginning of a project to establish a heritage trail throughout the ground, with themed memorabilia, a timeline and honours boards commemorating some of the golden moments and star names that have graced the historic ground in Leeds 6.

THEY SAID IT

'Many of the frustrations built up over 20 years fell away at the end of a ferocious contest that left even those in the safety of the stands feeling bruised and battered . . . for everyone at the Leeds club this will rank among their favourite memories.'

Independent **correspondent Dave Hadfield extols the Rhinos' 15–8 win over Wigan at usually unhappy hunting ground Central Park, in August 1998**

LICENSED TO THRILL

In 2008, the Rugby Football League took the revolutionary step of issuing three-year licences for clubs to play in Super League. This was as a replacement for straight promotion and relegation which was deemed to mitigate against the running of clubs as successful businesses, to give continuity and the chance to bring through greater numbers of youngsters for those in the elite. It also gave sides joining the necessary criteria to achieve before acceptance that would make them viable members of the competition. Every club, no matter what its standing, was required to submit a comprehensive application and was given a consequent grading. Leeds were one of three clubs – Warrington and Hull the others – deemed to be grade A standard, the report on them saying, 'An example of an older stadium that has had significant improvements, with more planned. The club has historic and projected profits and strong net assets. Commercially the club has produced good results and they achieve high attendances. The club's playing record speaks for itself and the club is producing quality Club Trained players.'

FIVE FINALS AT ELLAND ROAD

1) 1938 'All Leeds' Championship final v Hunslet – lost 8–2
Heartbreak for fans of the side north of the River Aire as the spoils, in a match that captivated the City like no other, went south to Parkside. Switched from Wakefield's Belle Vue, over 54,000 crammed into Elland Road – then the biggest rugby crowd in England.

2) 1983 John Player final v Wigan – lost 15–4
Strangely, the first ever final between the code's two most decorated names with both desperate to recapture former

glories. A superb try from Henderson Gill and a late one to Brian Juliff saw the cherry and whites home and hinted at their spell of unprecedented dominance that was to come.

3) 1988 Yorkshire Cup final v Castleford – won 33–12
A passionate crowd saw a match dominated by two interceptions at the start of each half from Garry Schofield and Carl Gibson, who both finished with try doubles. Australian Cliff Lyons won the White Rose Trophy for a consummate all-round display with Lee Crooks and Roy Powell also outstanding for Mal Reilly's men, against his former club.

4) 2005 World Club Challenge v Canterbury Bulldogs – won 39–32
The biggest British crowd ever for a World Club decider sold out Elland Road and witnessed a thriller as Leeds became the best side on the planet for the first time. After building a big lead playing some scintillating rugby, the Rhinos were indebted to Kevin Sinfield's calming drop goal.

5) 2008 World Club Challenge v Melbourne Storm – won 11–4
An epic clash in driving rain and howling wind which redefined the physical nature of sport, being the first match on British soil to contain 800 tackles. Matt Diskin and Dallas Johnson led the way with 60 each for their side, Leeds holding firm thanks to Scott Donald's try and Kevin Sinfield's majestic kicking.

SIX MEMORABLE HEADINGLEY MATCHES

25 January 1908 –
NORTHERN UNION 14 NEW ZEALAND 6
An occasion that selects itself on significance alone, the historic first ever 'Test' match played in front of just over 8,000 fans.

No Leeds players were in the NU line up but H.F. Rowe, the All Golds' centre, later signed for the Loiners.

25 April 1938 –
LEEDS 5 SWINTON 2,
Championship semi-final
With Hunslet already through to the title decider, over 29,000 fans packed Headingley on a Monday evening to see if Leeds could ensure the city's dream final. Despite being without seven regulars including Vic Hey and Jim Brough, and going into the final stages 2–0 down, Eric Harris conjured a scintillating 70-metre interception try to secure a momentous victory and live up to his nickname of the 'Toowoomba Ghost'.

7 November 1970 –
AUSTRALIA 12 GREAT BRITAIN 7,
World Cup final
Headingley staged the biggest game in the world which became the notorious 'battle of Leeds'. Fresh from having won the Ashes Down Under, GB were favourites having already beaten the Aussies in the group stages at the ground. A record six Leeds players – Smith, Hynes, Atkinson, Shoebottom, Fisher and Haigh – took the field for the national side in a game that was a mixture between chess and trench warfare; Atkinson scoring but Hynes being sent off as Father John Cootes' try won the cup.

19 March 1978 –
LEEDS 16 BRADFORD NORTHERN 8,
Challenge Cup quarter-final
An electrifying atmosphere created by 18,600 fans, who witnessed two contrasting halves of sensational football as Leeds moved a step nearer to retaining the Challenge Cup. After an incredibly tense, scoreless first half Bradford took the lead until John Atkinson produced one of his finest-ever long-range tries down the North Stand side after a blind-side

scrum move. He repeated the glorious feat soon after in a performance that summed up Leeds in the cup at their best.

19 July 1997 –
LEEDS RHINOS 22 ADELAIDE RAMS 14,
World Club Championship
The sunlit evening when summer rugby truly arrived at Headingley, and one of the few successes by an English club against their Australian counterparts. In a carnival atmosphere that was the precursor of the Friday night experience, over 11,000 shirt-sleeved fans thrilled to the modern reincarnation of the sport capped by a wonder try; Paul Sterling unforgettably going 100 metres down the South Stand side from a restart. The Rhinos side contained seven players who had come through the Academy, with Adrian Morley outstanding.

5 October 2007 –
LEEDS RHINOS 36 WIGAN WARRIORS 6,
Final Eliminator
The Rhinos produced a near-perfect performance to qualify for Old Trafford with an unprecedented 100 per cent completion rate in the first half. Brent Webb's wonder try from a colossal Jamie Peacock burst set the tone as the Warriors were put to the sword. Kevin Sinfield and Jamie Jones-Buchanan fashioned a similarly glorious score for Rob Burrow as Leeds gained the attacking confidence they took so gloriously into the following week's Grand Final.

LANDMARKS FOR LEEDS

1890 – The newly-founded Leeds Rugby Club, formed principally from the old St John's outfit, the 'amber and blues' of Cardigan Fields, beat Manningham in the first game played at Headingley.

1895 – Leeds headed to Leigh in the opening round of fixtures of the breakaway Northern Union, winning 6–3 with tries from Bastow and Parfitt.

1910 – The first silverware adorned the Headingley trophy cabinet as jubilant crowds greeted the side at Leeds station as they brought back the Challenge Cup, following a replay win over Hull at Huddersfield.

1932 – The first Rugby League match played under floodlights saw Leeds defeat Wigan 18–9 at White City in London.

1936 – Leeds made their first trip to Wembley and easily beat Warrington in the Challenge Cup final in front of a record British crowd of over 50,000, generating best-ever receipts of over £7,000.

1937 – Salford and Leeds were involved in a first for the sport when on Coronation Day, 12 May, they played an exhibition game of 12-a-side, Leeds winning 15–9.

1938 – On Christmas Eve, Vic Hey scored the only try ever to be posted on the cricket pitch as Leeds defeated Salford 5–0, the match being switched for the only time in history because the rugby pitch on the other side was frozen over.

1950 – Leeds helped generate the biggest ever semi-final crowd, as 69,898 saw Arthur Clues' men miss out on Wembley as Warrington won 16–4 at Odsal in the Challenge Cup.

1969 – Leeds were crowned European Champions, having defeated Perpignan 31–5 at Headingley.

1970 – Bob Haigh broke the record for the number of tries scored in a season by a forward, registering 40, the bulk of them from passes by Ray Batten.

1995 – Ellery Hanley set a new world record for a forward by scoring 41 tries in a season, the landmark touchdown coming in victory at Warrington.

1997 – Ronnie the Rhino made his first appearance at Headingley, eventually going on to stand as a Parliamentary candidate for the Headingley ward.

1999 – Leeds created the record for the highest score in a Challenge Cup final with a crushing defeat of London Broncos in the last Rugby League encounter played at the old Twin Towers, Lance Todd Trophy winner Leroy Rivett becoming the first player to score four tries in the decider.

2005 – The Rhinos were crowned World Champions as they defeated a Sonny Bill Williams-inspired Canterbury 39–32 in front of a sell-out crowd at Elland Road.

2006 – Dame Kelly Holmes helped launch the Leeds Rugby Foundation, the independent charitable trust established to run all Leeds Rugby's community activity.

2008 – Brian McClennan's side became the first to win the World Club Challenge and Super League in the same calendar year.

2009 – Leeds established themselves as the first team in the summer era to win three consecutive Grand Finals, all against St Helens.

NAILING THEIR COLOURS TO THE MAST

A group of the most colourful Loiners:

Gordon Brown
David Rose
R. Green
Brendan White
Richie Blackmore
Gavin Brown
Jason Golden
Jeff Grayshon
'Bluey' McClennan

UP FOR THE CUP

Leeds currently stand third in the list of most Challenge Cup wins, returning with the coveted silverware on 11 occasions from 20 final appearances. Wigan with 17 and St Helens 12 are the clubs above them.

Five Loiners have won the Lance Todd Trophy for a man of the match display in the decider, two of them when on the losing side. Scrum-half Jeff Stevenson was the first to be presented with the award, his busy display helping to overcome Barrow in 1957. Prop Steve Pitchford's blockbusting charges were germane to Leeds' underdog victory against Widnes 20 years later and Leroy Rivett's record four-try haul made him the obvious choice when London Broncos were overwhelmed in the second half in the last final at the old Wembley in 1999. Full-back Gary Connolly in 2003 and skipper Kevin Sinfield two years later were deemed the outstanding performers at Cardiff's Millennium Stadium although both would have gladly traded personal glory for team success.

Headingley has hosted 13 Challenge Cup finals, Batley winning the first three of them in 1897, 1898 and 1901. Huddersfield in 1913 and 1920 are the only other side to have won it more than once on the hallowed turf. Leeds have only appeared in a cup final at headquarters once, in the second leg of the 1943 competition. Although Dai Jenkins, Charlie Eaton and guest player Jack Walkington from Hunslet landed first half goals in a 6–0 win, it was not enough to overturn a first-leg deficit, Eddie Waring's Dewsbury winning 16–15 on aggregate. Warrington, Bradford, Wakefield, Dewsbury, Rochdale – the sole time they paraded the trophy – and Oldham were the other victors at Headingley who lifted the Fattorini-designed silver centrepiece.

1910 – Leeds were victorious in the first replay against Hull, Frank Young landing the most goals in a final with seven while Leeds' 26 points are the highest number scored in a final to date.

1923 – Loiners won the newly-named Rugby League Challenge Cup, again against Hull, in the only final to be played at Wakefield.

1932 – The final that Wembley forsook because the brought-forward date clashed with an England v Scotland football international. Moved to Wigan, Leeds faced a Swinton side that had not conceded a try in the earlier rounds. The only one they did, a touchline-hugging scorcher from Eric Harris, saw Leeds home.

1942 – Australian Test stand-off Vic Hey became the first Leeds captain to lift the cup twice, both times against Halifax, after scoring two game-turning tries in 1941. The following year, Jim Brough came out of retirement after three years away, at the age of 38, to turn in a man of the match performance.

1943 – Leeds lost the first two-legged final by a point over Easter. Alan Edwards, a guest three-quarter from Salford, scored twice for Leeds in 1942 but grabbed the opening touchdown against them a year later.

1947 – Leeds reached the final without conceding a point but could not replicate that form against derby rivals Bradford at the Empire Stadium in front of a world record attendance at any Rugby League match of 77,605.

1957 – Having had a record-breaking season, eventually amassing 496 points, Lewis Jones failed to kick a goal at Wembley as Barrow were beaten 9–7, one of only two games where he was not on the score sheet that year.

1968 – Best remembered for the 'Watersplash' final and Don Fox's heartbreaking late miss for Wakefield, Leeds produced a near-perfect performance in the semi-final to blow Wigan away, 25–4, at Station Road, Swinton.

1971 – Syd Hynes ignominiously became the first player to be sent off at Wembley – by Billy Thompson – after clashing with Alex Murphy in the 65th minute, as his side went down to massive underdogs Leigh. Subsequently, Richie Eyres – who was later to play for Leeds – joined him in the black book in 1993.

1972 – Leeds conceded the earliest try recorded in a final when Keith Hepworth's hurried kick was charged down after 26 seconds by Graham Rees, who re-gathered to score.

1977 – After the tragic death of scrum-half Chris Sanderson, Kevin Dick played his first cup tie in the final, performing a key role with three goals, a cheeky dummy for a try and a drop goal as 'Cup Kings' Widnes were turned over.

1978 – Leeds retained the trophy with the greatest comeback in history, which stood until 1996. Having gone 10 points down in as many minutes and 12–5 behind at the break, John Holmes with a seemingly impossible drop goal, capped a sensational revival.

1982 – The cruellest of defeats at Swinton saw the Loiners miss out on Wembley when Widnes' Mick Adams launched a speculative punt with the last kick of the semi-final. It came back off the crossbar and into the arms of Keiron O'Loughlin for the winning try.

1994 – Aged 17 years 200 days, Francis Cummins became the youngest player to appear and score a try at Wembley, his long-range effort not enough to quell Wigan for whom Martin Offiah scored one of the best tries ever seen at the stadium.

1995 – Leeds and Wigan became the first clubs to meet in consecutive Wembley finals, having surprisingly avoided each other in the previous near-century of finals. Ellery Hanley played what turned out to be his last domestic game, the Leeds skipper powerless to prevent his old club retaining the trophy.

1999 – The Rhinos ran in the highest score and widest margin in a final as London Broncos were eventually swept aside. Leeds posted the equal most tries scored – 9 (with Huddersfield in 1915) – while Iestyn Harris equalled the goals and points in a final tally, with 8 and 20 respectively.

2000 – Leeds qualified to defend the trophy for the first of the 'on the road' finals while Wembley was rebuilt and, following the success of a Super League fixture in Edinburgh the year before, the RFL took the decider to Scotland for the first time. There was drama on the Thursday before when the ground and changing rooms were submerged under 3ft of water, but battle still commenced.

2003 – The only semi-final to go into extra time saw Leeds defeat St Helens 33–26 in one of the best knockout matches the sport had seen; youngster Danny McGuire the two-try hero off the bench. Victory saw the side through to Cardiff and the inaugural final played 'indoors' when the Millennium Stadium roof was shut.

2005 – A year before the introduction of Catalans Dragons, French opposition in the cup is like buses when, having not previously faced Gallic flair, two sides came along in the same season. Pia were defeated at Headingley and Toulouse in the semi-final, the Rhinos winning 126–18 across the games. Victory against Justin Morgan's men saw the Rhinos play in the first August final.

SETTING THE COURSE

The arrival of revolutionary Welshman Roy Francis in 1963 to take the reins heralded the start of coaches having a major impact and profile at Headingley. His innovative methods, centred principally on fitness, speed and ball movement, occasioned the second golden era at the club, cementing the foundations for a period of unprecedented silverware-gathering. He was succeeded by 'A' team coach Jack Nelson who had been a mentor to a number of the local youngsters who provided the core of the team but he tragically passed away over Christmas 1968, leaving the club shell-shocked and Joe Warham in caretaker charge for the remainder of the Championship-winning season until Derek Turner took over until 1973. His surprise sacking saw the arrival of an icon of the sport, former Wigan great Eric Ashton taking his turn at the tiller and although he claimed that it was the most enjoyable year of his hugely successful coaching career, the travelling from St Helens proved to be too onerous. That saw the return of the legendary Francis – who had initially departed for North Sydney where his regime was highly coveted – for a season, taking a young side to Premiership glory. Since then, Leeds have had 14 coaches in 35 years – Maurice Bamford having two spells in the hot seat – although in the turbulent 1980s they had 8 different supremos searching for success, the uncertainty at the helm no doubt in part accounting for the inconsistency seen in battle. Perhaps the most surprising appointment was that of Bradford's Peter Fox whose arrival was seen by many as akin to that of Brian Clough at neighbouring Elland Road. His teams had always played in a style antithetical to that demanded by the entertainment-conscious Headingley faithful who prided flamboyance over pragmatism. Five of these modern era coaches also played for the club; Syd Hynes, Robin Dewhurst, David Ward, Dean Bell and Daryl Powell. Malcolm Reilly who had held the reins in the late 1980s, memorably winning the Yorkshire Cup at Elland Road against his former side Castleford, returned in 2001 as an assistant to Daryl Powell, leaving two years later.

At the helm for Leeds in the modern era

1963–8	Roy Francis – left for North Sydney
1968	Jack Nelson – passed away
1969	Joe Warhan – caretaker
1969–73	Derek Turner – sacked
1973–4	Eric Ashton – left for St Helens
1974–5	Roy Francis – left for Bradford
1975–81	Syd Hynes – stood down
1981–3	Robin Dewhurst – sacked
1983–5	Maurice Bamford – left for Great Britain

1985	Malcolm Clift – contract not renewed
1985–6	Peter Fox – sacked
1986–8	Maurice Bamford – sacked
1988–9	Malcolm Reilly – left for Great Britain
1989–91	David Ward – sacked
1991–5	Doug Laughton – stood down
1995–7	Dean Bell – became Head of Youth Development
1997–9	Graham Murray – moved to Sydney Roosters
1999–2001	Dean Lance – sacked
2001–3	Daryl Powell – became Head of Youth Development
2004–7	Tony Smith – left for Great Britain
2007–	Brian McClennan

CLUB SCORING RECORDS

Most tries in a career

Eric Harris (winger, Australian) – 391 (1930–9)
John Atkinson (winger, English) – 342 (1966–82)
Alan Smith (winger, English) – 283 (1962–83)
Drew Turnbull (winger, Scottish) – 228 (1948–56)
Les Dyl (centre, English) – 193 (1970–85)

Current squad
Danny McGuire (stand-off, English) – 163
Keith Senior (centre, English) – 157
Rob Burrow (scrum-half, English) – 123

Most tries in a season

63 – Eric Harris (1935–6)
58 – Eric Harris (1930–1)
57 – Eric Harris (1932–3)

45 – Eric Harris (1934–5)
44 – Wilf Rosenberg (winger, South African 1960–1)

Most tries in a match

8 – Fred Webster (prop, English, v Coventry home 12/4/1912 won 102–0)
8 – Eric Harris (v Bradford home 14/9/1931 won 75–18)
7 – Eric Harris (v Acton & Willesden away 20/4/1936 won 54–5)
6 – Eric Harris (v Featherstone away 24/2/1937 won 36–10)
6 – Drew Turnbull (v Batley home 28/12/1953 won 44–5)
6 – Del Hodgkinson (winger, English, v Huddersfield home Yorkshire Cup 30/8/1958 won 64–17)

Most tries in a Super League match

5 – Ryan Hall (winger, English, v Castleford home 14/9/2009 won 76–12)
5 – Ali Lauitiiti (second-row, New Zealand, v Wakefield away 10/6/2005 won 70–6)
5 – Danny McGuire (v Widnes home 11/6/2004 won 48–24)

Most goals in a career (including drop goals)

1,244 – Lewis Jones (centre/stand-off, Welsh 1952–64)
1,119 – Kevin Sinfield (loose forward, English 1997–)
862 – Joe Thompson (prop, English 1923–33)
611 – Bev Risman (full-back, English 1966–70)
601 – Iestyn Harris (full-back/stand-off, Welsh, 1997–2001)

Most goals in a season (including drop goals)

168 – Iestyn Harris (1999)
166 – Lewis Jones (1956–7)
165 – Bev Risman (1968–9)
163 – Bev Risman (1966–7)
159 – John Holmes (full-back, English 1970–1)

Most goals in a match

17 – Iestyn Harris (v Swinton away Challenge Cup 11/2/2001 won 106–10)

13 – Iestyn Harris (v Huddersfield home 16/7/1999 won 86–6)

13 – Lewis Jones (v Blackpool home 19/8/1957 won 68–5)

Most points in a career

2,920 – Lewis Jones

2,261* – Kevin Sinfield (* to end 2009 season)

1,883 – Joe Thompson

1,554 – John Holmes

1,455 – Iestyn Harris

Most points in a season

431 – Lewis Jones (1956–7)

414 – Iestyn Harris (1999)

347 – Bev Risman (1966–7)

Most points in a match

42 – Iestyn Harris (v Huddersfield home 16/7/1999 – 4 tries, 13 goals)

38 – Iestyn Harris (v Swinton away Challenge Cup 11/2/2001 – 1 try, 17 goals)

31 – Lewis Jones (v Bradford away, won 40–14 – 3 tries, 11 goals)

30 – Mick Shoebottom (v Batley away, won 39–11 – 4 tries, 9 goals)

29 – Lewis Jones (v Blackpool home 19/8/1957 – 1 try, 13 goals)

FIRST OVERSEAS SIGNINGS

Leeds signed two Kiwi three-quarters as their first overseas players, both of whom had come over on the inaugural 'All Golds' tour of 1907/8, although they arrived at Headingley a year apart. Canterbury's Joe Lavery, a railwayman who was 27 when he toured, made his debut at Broughton Rangers in the opening game of the 1908/9 campaign in what was to be one of only ten appearances for the club. He scored his debut try in the derby with Hunslet at home, failing to prevent a 13–10 defeat and in all crossed four times for the club, all of them coming in October in the space of as many matches, including a brace against Hull. Harold Rowe, an accountant from Auckland who was equally adept at full-back, wing or centre took Lavery's place the following season, the pair having played together as centres against Keighley on that historic, inaugural tour. Rowe was something of a celebrity, having played in the very first Northern Union international against Wales in Aberdare and then in the opening Test against England, staged at Headingley. Albert Baskiville's 'All Gold' tourists had been based in the Grand Central Hotel in Leeds for a section of their tour – and they had also resided at Ilkley's Hydro – and the players gained a particular affinity for the city which prompted the desire of the pair to return to try their hand in the club game. They were particularly impressed with Leeds' 'grand, imposing architecture, avenues and parks and endless variety of shows and entertainment,' according to contemporary reports. Rowe played 32 times in all for the Loiners, crossing for 12 tries, his first in a narrow victory at Lawkholme Lane of all places. He subsequently scored in five consecutive games, including the sole touchdown in a 5–0 home win over Hull Kingston Rovers. His greatest moment came as part of the first Leeds team to win the Challenge Cup, in a replayed final against Hull at Huddersfield. Although not included in the first game, Jimmy Sanders' serious injury necessitated a reshuffle of the back line, which saw Jimmy Fawcett moved to half-back and Rowe drafted in for the Monday afternoon rematch. He set up the first try for Fred Webster, being hauled down just short from a scrum before his crowning glory came at the start of the second half. He was on hand to back up breaks by Ware and Gillie to score Leeds' fifth touchdown, behind the posts, of a memorable, record-breaking win. His last try for the club was scored in a big home win over York at the start of the following season but, a month later with the Leeds backs out of form and frequent injury absence a growing concern, he was transferred to Rochdale. Stalwart John 'Dinny' Campbell, who went on to play 258 times in the colours, was the first Australian to sign for the club. Arriving from Penrith, he made his debut at home to Keighley in September 1912, scoring his first try at Bramley two weeks later.

THEY SAID IT

'Looking back, 48 matches in a season was far too many but it was the norm in those days and you got on with it. As a player you are paid to play rugby, you are not there to ponce about looking good.'

Captain fantastic David Ward looks back on his time in the blue and amber

SPLASHING THE CASH

While it has never been a scientifically proven process, the breaking of transfer records has brought publicity and profile to the sport, kudos to the buyer and provided a reputation to live up to for the target in question. The first time Leeds hit the headlines in the market was in 1921 when they were purportedly involved in the first £1,000 transfer when they snared winger Harold Buck from neighbours Hunslet. There were unconfirmed reports at the time that another player moved with Buck to Headingley thereby reducing the figure but a significant barrier had been broken, whether a publicity stunt or not. There was no doubting the fee when Leeds broke the record twice more as they began to build their first great side of the 1930s.

Another international winger, Stanley Smith, moved from Wakefield during the 1929 Test series against the Kangaroos for £1,075. Three years later, Stanley Brogden followed him from Huddersfield for an extra £125. Leeds were record sellers for the first time in 1949 when loose forward Ike Owens went to Castleford for a short spell before moving on to Huddersfield for the same £2,750 fee. Leeds were back at the top of the scale in 1950 when enticing burly Australian winger Bruce Ryan from Hull for £4,750, although again his tenure was short. They were involved in a record deal for Hunslet loose forward Brian Shaw in 1961 but the figure of £13,250 for the deal included Bernard Prior, valued at £3,500 and Norman Burton, deemed to be worth £250 who made their way to Parkside.

It was just over 25 years before Leeds again rewrote the cheque books, in a reaction to nearly being relegated for the first time. Twice in quick succession they raised the bar, raiding financially ailing Hull on both occasions for two players who could not have moved in more contrasting fashion. Airlie Bird, local hero, prop Lee Crooks made no secret of his displeasure at being used as a financial pawn when he arrived for £150,000 closely followed by prodigal son Garry Schofield who joined his home city club for £5,000 more. In 1991, as Leeds desperately sought to hang on to the coat-tails of full-time Wigan, who were sweeping all before them, Leeds brought Central Park talisman Ellery Hanley to the place of his birth as captain and assistant coach for a cool £250,000, money that was in part recouped by consecutive trips to Wembley under his stewardship. Leeds broke that record, although not the code's highest, as Martin Offiah's move to Wigan had almost doubled the Hanley fee a year later, when they captured Iestyn Harris from Warrington in 1997. Although listed at £350,000, the deal included Academy youngster Danny Sculthorpe crossing to Wilderspool with the young prop valued at £25,000. Harris had initially been listed at a staggering £1,350,000 when put on the market almost a year earlier.

The record fee paid by a lower division club came to Leeds in 1996 when Huddersfield agreed to hand over £135,000 for Garry Schofield who left to become their player-coach. Moves from rugby union are even less quantifiable with no fee involved, just a payment to the player concerned, which both parties are unlikely to have fully revealed. Leeds were believed to have paid the most ever for a convert as they shocked both codes by snapping up the then 15-a-side player of the year when they announced the arrival of All Black full-back John Gallagher. That was for a reported £350,000, five-year deal in 1990, although he joined London Crusaders after only three troubled seasons. Conversely, when Iestyn Harris moved to rugby union with Cardiff in 2001, it was reportedly for a £2 million, four-year package, in concert with the Welsh RU. Rugby League's most itinerant player, Geoff Clarkson, spent three seasons at Leeds from 1973 to 1975, making 66 appearances. It was his longest spell at any of the ten clubs – involving a record twelve transfers – he featured for in a 17-year career that saw him eventually hang up his boots at the age of 40.

FAIR PLAY

In 2007, as Leeds began their unprecedented monopoly of Super League titles, Featherstone-based bathroom suppliers Frontline joined up with the RFL to institute a Fair Play Index and accompanying award with cash prize. Based on five categories of misdemeanour, the 'cleanest' side took the honours. Despite dominating on the field, the Rhinos have not been in contention for this particular accolade. Points are picked up on the following basis with the idea being to keep them to a minimum:

1 point – Technical penalty
2 points – Foul play penalty
3 points – Sin-binning
4 points – Sending off sufficient
5 points – For each match of a ban

Leeds in the Frontline Index
2007 – Finished 7th on 330 points – winners Harlequins 268 points
2008 – Finished 4th on 310 points – winners St Helens 222 points
2009 – Finished 11th on 263 points – winners Hull 186 points

KEEPING WARM

After the big freeze of 1962 into the early weeks of 1963, which saw Headingley without a game for a staggering four months – between 1 December and 3 April – the decision was taken by the Board to install under soil heating. The 'blanket' was made up of 38 miles of cable positioned 6 inches from the surface. Wired in April 1963 at a cost of £6,488, it was calculated that the bill to have it on for a period of 24 hours was in the region of £300, however such initiative paid for itself many times over. It was first used on 21 December 1963 when Dewsbury won 8–4. Matches, especially cup ties, were moved to the ground as play was guaranteed and the BBC made Headingley almost a permanent home, safe in the knowledge that scheduled games – especially on Boxing Day – would go ahead. When the next harsh winter came, in 1979, Leeds played all their home matches as fixtured and sat back while others played catch-up late in the season, enabling them to triumph in the Premiership. After almost forty years, the degenerating system was dug up in March 2002 after it was deemed that the compacting of the soil had led to drainage problems.

COUNTY'S FINEST

Before the great split in 1895, the Yorkshire Cup held a position of pre-eminence in the rugby calendar, drawing massive crowds, having huge prestige and, to some extent, proving that there was a real appetite among players and fans for more formalised competition. Ten years after the breakaway, the Northern Union instituted their own version and, in the White Rose county, Leeds were pre-eminent both on the field and with Headingley as the venue for the decider. In all, the Loiners contested 21 Yorkshire Cup finals, winning 17 of them, holding records for the highest score in 1972 when they beat Dewsbury 36–9 at Bradford, and most goals when David Stephenson booted six at Elland Road when Castleford were vanquished in 1988. The Great Britain centre became one of the few players to own a winners' medal in every competition available on that memorable afternoon in front of 23,000 fans. Leeds were also on the end of a high watermark, Huddersfield's

Stan Moorhouse scoring four tries as his side triumphed 24–5 at Halifax in 1919. Introduced in 1966 to reward the man of the match, eight Leeds players won the White Rose Trophy – organised by the Yorkshire Federation of Supporters' Clubs – before the competition was disbanded in 1992, the most by any side in that period. All were backs; Barry Seabourne (1968 v Castleford), John Holmes (1972 v Dewsbury), Keith Hepworth (1973 v Wakefield), Les Dyl (1976 v Featherstone), Alan Smith (1979 v Halifax), Kevin Dick (1980 v Hull K.R.) and the sole overseas player among the octet, Aussie Cliff Lyons (1988 v Castleford).

The biggest attendance at a Yorkshire Cup final was in 1949 when 36,000 fans packed Headingley to see Bradford beat Huddersfield 11–4. That was one of 46 finals played at the stadium, one – between Bradford and Castleford in 1987 – ending in a 12–12 draw, the replay being staged at Elland Road. The side with the best record at Headingley in those games is, perhaps surprisingly, Leeds, who won all four of the games they appeared in on their own ground when sponsors in the 1970s, Esso, decided that it was their preferred venue, irrespective of who contested the final. Huddersfield and Bradford found the turf to their liking, winning two-thirds of the deciders they played in there. Conversely, Hull must have detested the choice, losing three-quarters of the time they appeared at Headingley in a record 15 visits, Batley having a similarly depressing ratio and Featherstone the worst success rate, winning only once in six visits.

Yorkshire Cup finals at Headingley – win/lose ratio (46 matches)

Huddersfield	W 8	L 3	
Bradford	W 6	L 2	D 1
Hull K.R.	W 6	L 3	
Wakefield	W 5	L 4	
Leeds	W 4	L 0	

York	W 3	L 2	
Castleford	W 3	L 3	D 1
Hull	W 3	L12	
Halifax	W 2	L 2	
Hunslet	W 2	L 4	
Dewsbury	W 1	L 1	
Batley	W 1	L 4	
Featherstone	W 1	L 5	

PUTTING THEIR BODIES ON THE LINE

Top ten body-related exponents:

Eric Grothe
R. Boagey
Kevin Dick
Cliff Whitehead
Toe-knee Smith
Ikram Butt
Paddy Handley
Des Armitage
Ian Payne

RUGBY LEAGUE RECORDS

All-time records in the code currently held by Leeds players:

Most points in a season
496 – Lewis Jones (1956/7)

Made up as follows: 48 appearances, 194 goals, 36 tries
For Leeds – 431 points (43 appearances, 166 goals, 33 tries)
Comprised of:
League matches – 36 appearances, 147 goals, 30 tries
Challenge Cup – 5 appearances, 13 goals, 2 tries

Yorkshire Cup – 1 appearance, 3 goals, 1 try
Play-off – 1 appearance, 3 goals

For GB – 51 points (3 appearances, 21 goals, 3 tries)
For Rest – 8 points (1 appearance, 4 goals)
For RL XIII – 6 points (1 appearance, 3 goals)

The iconic Welshman also holds the record for number of points and goals scored on tour with Great Britain when visiting Australia and New Zealand in 1954, totalling 278 from 127 goals and 8 tries, garnered in 21 matches.

Consecutive run of try-scoring matches
17 matches, totalling 36 tries – Eric Harris (1935/6)

From 7 December – with a hat-trick at home to Batley – through to 29 February when he crossed against York at Headingley, winger Eric Harris crossed for at least one try. He scored nine hat-tricks during the season, equalling the club record he set five years earlier, part of a total of 42 occasions when he got over the whitewash three times or more, easily another Headingley best.

Most appearances for Great Britain
Garry Schofield jointly holds the record for Great Britain appearances alongside winger Mick Sullivan, totalling 46. All of Sullivan's were starting performances while two of Schofield's came off the bench.

Although Leeds-born, Schofield began his representative career while at Hull, completing the record after moving to his home city club in 1987 and appearing in the national shirt 31 times while at Headingley. By touring four times, in 1984, 1988, 1990 and 1992, he created another landmark for the sport.

Most goals for Great Britain

The highest number of goals kicked for Great Britain in a game, 10, is shared by five players, two of them from Leeds. Lewis Jones was the first to achieve the feat, against Australia in Brisbane in 1954. John Holmes equalled it in a World Cup game in Pau against New Zealand in 1972. He also scored two tries for a total of 26 points which was a record until broken by another former Leeds player, Bobbie Goulding, 24 years later.

Oldest Great Britain player

Veteran prop Jeff Grayshon was 36 years, 8 months and 4 days old when he won his last of 13 caps against New Zealand at Elland Road on 9 November 1985.

ICON OF A GENERATION 3 – LEWIS JONES

On seven occasions, Leeds have broken the world record for transfer fees between clubs but arguably the best bit of business they ever did was to pay a then unparalleled £6,000, in 1954, to a 21-year-old Welshman and British Lion, who was the darling of the rugby union public in the Principality. His capture by the Loiners – a club renowned for travelling the extra mile to snare the very best – was as surprising and astonishing as it was shocking. Austerity was still the vogue in 1952 when Lewis hurriedly swapped South Wales for North Leeds – his unprecedented signing-on fee was enough to buy three houses. For that he carried the epithet 'Golden Boy' but the reference to the precious metal equally applied to his talent. Exactly 45 years after he hung up his metronomic boots at Headingley, Lewis Jones remains the darling of an era, his talents still whispered of in reverential terms and viewed by many as the greatest player ever to pull on the famous blue and amber colours. Variously described as a genius and enigma, unique or infuriating, he attracted 17,000 fans to Headingley for his debut. After an early badly broken arm at Batley, which threatened to permanently derail his new career, he was never anything other than top box office and went on to set a host of points scoring records. He remains the highest points scorer and most prolific goal-kicker in the history of the club while his official seasonal total of 496 in 1956/7 is still the greatest haul the sport has seen. He was a master footballer guaranteeing virtually 8 points every time he set foot on a field. With ball in hand, there have been few finer; his hitch kick, floated pass and disguised scissors have gone into Headingley folk lore. Fans marvelled at his ability to create space for others or to exploit the merest hint of a chance with his acceleration and glide. Seemingly unflappable, elegant, quiet, intense and a wonderful sportsman, he carved his everlasting niche in Loiners folklore when captaining the side to their first ever Championship victory in 1961, fittingly scoring the final try at Odsal, where – with Don Robinson – the pair became the first Leeds players to hold cup and title winners' medals. At various times a car salesman, groundsman and shopkeeper, he returned from a highly successful player-coaching spell in Australia – where he steered Wentworthville to five Second Division premierships and posted over 1,000 more points – to train as a maths teacher, taking up a post at Silver Royd Girls High School. He coached the Leeds 'A' team for a season and briefly held the reins at Dewsbury.

VINTAGE YEARS & DARK DAYS

1901/2

Leeds, buoyed by the inclusion of eight players from the recently disbanded Leeds Parish Church side and as members of the Yorkshire Senior Competition, brought the first silverware to the club, completely transforming their hitherto dismal Northern Union fortunes. Having averaged barely three points a game two seasons before, the side, which included a host of other new signings, went on a record-breaking run that saw them head the table. Although losing two (at York and Holbeck) and drawing one (away to Keighley) of their first seven fixtures, the Loiners then went on an unprecedented stint of success, remaining unbeaten throughout the remainder of the campaign, a total of 20 matches. The only dropped point was a draw at Heckmondwike as the side were all-conquering at home for the first time winning all 14 league clashes and a Northern Union cup tie against Windhill. Former Oldham centre T.D. Davies set a record of 19 touchdowns, becoming the first Leeds player to score three hat-tricks in a season. At home to Heckmondwike he crossed four times but scrum-half G. Grace beat him to it a week before against Castleford at Headingley in the club's biggest ever win, 36–2. Celebrating winning the shield, accepted by captain supreme, stand-off George Mosley (one of the Parish Eight), Leeds beat 'The Rest' 7–5 at home, winger F. Mudd, formerly of Hunslet, scoring the Leeds try and Mosley securing the win with a touchline conversion.

1945/6

Merely playing again after the ravages of war on populace and team alike, the first full season after the cessation of hostilities was a traumatic one for the Loiners. They won only one of their first nine league matches (although they did make the semi-final of the Yorkshire Cup during October), the nadir being four days in September when they suffered their worst away and then home defeats, both to local rivals. Wakefield began the rot, running in 17 tries in a 71–0 success at Belle Vue, which is still the biggest losing margin in a Leeds away game. Bradford then took advantage of the disarray to record a

54–3 victory at Headingley, taking the try tally conceded to 31 as opposed to a single reply from Eric Hesketh. The Wakefield loss remained a club record hammering until the Premiership semi-final at Wigan in May 1992 when Martin Offiah ran in 10 tries as Leeds were humbled 74–6. It took until the Queensland tourists arrived in 1983 for the home worst to be bettered, the Maroons trouncing their hosts 58–2. From 10 November to 26 January, the only point Leeds picked up was from a 7–7 draw at home to Hull, a total of 12 matches, setting unwanted highs for the number of consecutive games lost (10), home defeats (6) and away setbacks (12). Loiners' final league record of 26 defeats in 36 games remains their least impressive return, as does their 23rd-place finish out of 27 in one division rugby.

FIVE FANTASTIC SUMMER TOUCHDOWNS

1) Wayne McDonald
(v St Helens, away, April 2003 – won 24–16)
An almost surreal moment as the Rhinos replacement prop careered 70 metres downfield throwing two dummies to bamboozle the Saints defence and his own team-mates on a wonder charge.

2) Danny McGuire
(v Catalans, home, October 2009 – won 27–20)
A try worthy of a side reaching a Grand Final, Kevin Sinfield's long pass freed Scott Donald, whose beautifully weighted chip to the middle on half way saw Danny McGuire judge the holding wind and his catch to perfection before sprinting away from Adam Mogg.

3) Jamie Thackray
(v Catalans, away, February 2007 – lost 30–22)
Although ultimately in vain, this solo score had Jamie Thackray labelled 'le Wayne Rooney de Leeds' by the admiring French journalists. Taking the ball 40 metres out, the prop twice chipped over the cover and re-gathered, to claim a glorious, unexpected touchdown.

4) Rob Burrow
(v Canterbury Bulldogs, Elland Road, February 2005 – won 39–32)
Eight men handled in a bewildering array of inter-passing – Andrew Dunemann set Kevin Sinfield on the runaround with Ali Lauitiiti, Danny McGuire realeased the ever-willing Richard Mathers as the link, Gareth Ellis ranged out wide to feed Keith Senior whose inside ball freed Marcus Bai, his lob being collected by Rob Burrow for a breathtaking score.

5) Scott Donald
(v St Helens, Old Trafford, October 2007 – won 33–6)
As good a touchdown as has been seen in any final. From a restart, Brent Webb exploited the blind side and Keith Senior's snap pass sent Scott Donald clear down the left, his pace and swerve leaving Paul Wellens for dead on the outside for a classic winger's try.

THEY PAID THEIR MONEY

Attendance records at Headingley Carnegie Stadium:

Test Match
v Australia – 36,529 (9 October, 1948 – Great Britain 23 Australia 21)

v New Zealand – 28,445 (4 October, 1947 – Great Britain 11 New Zealand 10)
v France – 21,948 (14 March, 1959 – Great Britain 50 France 15)

League Match
v Bradford Northern – 40,175 (21 May, 1947 – draw 2–2)

Challenge Cup tie
v Wigan – 38, 914 (9 February, 1957 – won 13–11)

Super League
v Bradford Bulls – 23,035 (8 August, 2003 – lost 18–16)

Championship final
22,586 (4 May, 1968 – Wakefield 17 Hull K.R. 10)

Challenge Cup final
34,700 (29 April, 1922 – Rochdale 10 Hull 9)

Yorkshire Cup final
36,000 (29 October, 1949 – Bradford 11 Huddersfield 4)

NATIONAL TREASURES

When Great Britain was last triumphant in an Ashes Series in 1970, Leeds sent their highest number of tourists to date. Five Loiners made the trip Down Under, all of them backs, John Atkinson and Syd Hynes scoring tries in the 2–1 series victory over the Green and Golds while versatile Mick Shoebottom played in three different positions in each of the encounters. The total number of travellers was bettered in 1988, although half of the blue and amber contingent – Lee Crooks, Garry Schofield and Paul Medley – all came home early after suffering injuries and had to be replaced.

Leeds Lions

1910 – 3 tourists – Billy Ward, Fred Webster, Frank Young
1914 – 2 tourists – Willie A. Davies, Billy Jarman
1920 – 3 tourists – Jim Bacon, George Rees, Squire Stockwell
1924 – 2 tourists – Jim Bacon, Joe Thompson
1928 – 3 tourists – Jim Brough, Mel Rosser, Joe Thompson
1932 – 4 tourists – Les Adams, John Lowe, Stan Smith, Joe Thompson
1936 – 4 tourists – Stan Brogden, Jim Brough, Fred Harris, Stan Smith
1946 – 2 tourists – Dai Jenkins, Ike Owens
1950 – 1 tourist – Dickie Williams
1954 – 2 tourists – Lewis Jones, Drew Turnbull
1966 – 2 tourists – Harry Poole, Geoff Wrigglesworth
1970 – 5 tourists – John Atkinson, Syd Hynes, Barry Seabourne, Mick Shoebottom, Alan Smith
1974 – 3 tourists – John Atkinson, Les Dyl, Bill Ramsey
1979 – 2 tourists – John Holmes, David Ward
1984 – 1 tourist – Keith Rayne
1988 – 6 tourists – Lee Crooks, Carl Gibson, Paul Medley, Roy Powell, Garry Schofield, David Stephenson
1990 – 4 tourists – Paul Dixon, Carl Gibson, Roy Powell, Garry Schofield
1992 – 2 tourists – Ellery Hanley, Garry Schofield
1996 – 2 tourists – Neil Harmon, Adrian Morley
1999 Tri-Nations – 7 tourists – Francis Cummins, Iestyn Harris, Andy Hay, Barrie McDermott, Adrian Morley, Keith Senior, Ryan Sheridan
2006 Tri-Nations – 5 tourists – Rob Burrow, Gareth Ellis, Danny McGuire, Jamie Peacock, Keith Senior

- Joe Thompson was the first forward to make three tours.
- As well as playing on two tours, eight years apart, Jim Brough coached the Lions in 1958 to their best ever

record of 27 wins and a draw from 30 matches, scoring the most number of points.

- Three Loiners, Jim Brough, Harry Poole and Ellery Hanley, have been tour skippers although the latter lasted only nine minutes of his first match and was replaced as captain by club-mate Garry Schofield.
- Fred Webster, Willie Davies, John Atkinson (1970) and Roy Powell, twice have played the most games on tour; Lewis Jones (24 in 1966) and Syd Hynes (19 in 1970) were the leading try-scorers.

World Cup Representatives

Great Britain 1954 (winners) – Gordon Brown, David Rose
Great Britain 1957 – Lewis Jones, Jeff Stevenson
Great Britain 1968 – John Atkinson, Mick Clark, Bev Risman, Mick Shoebottom
Great Britain 1970 – John Atkinson, Tony Fisher, Bob Haigh, Syd Hynes, Mick Shoebottom, Alan Smith
Great Britain 1972 (winners) – John Atkinson, Terry Clawson, John Holmes, David Jeanes
England 1975 – John Atkinson, Phil Cookson, Les Dyl, John Holmes
Wales 1975 – Tony Fisher
Great Britain 1977 – Les Dyl, John Holmes, Steve Pitchford, David Ward
Great Britain 1985-8 – David Creasser, Jeff Grayshon, Paul Medley, Roy Powell
Great Britain 1985-92 – Paul Dixon, Phil Ford, Carl Gibson, Roy Powell, Garry Schofield
England 1995 – Paul Cook
Wales 1995 – Richie Eyres
New Zealand 1995 – Kevin Iro, Tony Kemp
Tonga 1995 – George Mann
England 2000 – Darren Fleary, Andy Hay, Adrian Morley, Keith Senior, Kevin Sinfield, Chev Walker

Ireland 2000 – David Barnhill, Jamie Mathiou, Barrie McDermott, Ryan Sheridan
New Zealand 2000 – Richie Blackmore
Scotland 2000 – Graham Mackay, Scott Rhodes
Wales 2000 – Garreth Carvell, Anthony Farrell, Iestyn Harris, Paul Sterling
England 2008 – Rob Burrow, Gareth Ellis, Jamie Jones-Buchanan, Danny McGuire, Jamie Peacock, Keith Senior, Kevin Sinfield, Lee Smith
France 2008 – Eric Anselme
Samoa 2008 – Ali Lauitiiti, Kylie Leuluai

- In the inaugural tournament in Paris, Gordon Brown scored two tries in Great Britain's 16–12 success over France.
- Bev Risman skippered the 1968 squad even though it contained his Leeds captain Mick Clark and, similarly, Jamie Peacock was the leader 40 years later even though Kevin Sinfield donned the mantle at club level.
- In six World Cup matches played at Headingley, Great Britain/England have only lost once, in the notorious final against Australia in 1970. The Aussies (also in 1970 in a group match), France (1975), South Africa (1995), Fiji (2000) and Ireland (in the quarter-final in 2000) were all vanquished. The only other World Cup match played there was in 1960 when Australia beat New Zealand 21–15.

OTHER NATIONALITIES

Post the 2008 World Cup debacle for England, talk turned to the re-formation of an Other Nationalities side, composed of the best players plying their trade in Super League from overseas. It was felt by many that such a quality composite outfit could provide the bridging layer of intense competition needed for aspiring international players more akin to the Southern Hemisphere's State of Origin. If resurrected, that would be the fourth such incarnation with the ONs having played 21 games, 16 against England – two of them at Headingley in 1924 and five years later – and five versus Wales. Leeds' Australian Arthur Clues and Kiwi Bert Cook were stalwarts of the sides in the late 1940s and early '50s. The very first representative game, on 5 April 1904 at Wigan's Central Park, was between England and Other Nationalities, a side made up of mainly Welshmen in a 12-a-side contest. Leeds provided two players, both for the Select outfit, in club record try-scorer T. Llewellyn and forward J. Moffat, as the 'visitors' won 9–3. The first clash under 13-a-side between the teams was scheduled for New Years' Day 1907 at Headingley but was postponed. In Australia, the Other Nationalities concept was tried only once, in 1964 for a game against Sydney Colts as a curtain-raiser to the Third Test against France at the SCG. Included in the foreigners' ranks were three former Leeds players on stints Down Under; Lewis Jones (Wentworthville) and centre pairing Derek Hallas (Parramatta) and Fred Pickup (Manly).

PRIDE OF YORKSHIRE

As well as a county cup competition, from 1895/6 to 1901/2 the senior clubs were split into county leagues, known as the respective Senior Competitions. Leeds were winners of the

Yorkshire Senior Cup for the sole time on the last of those seasons. Then, from 1907/8 until 1969/70, county League Championships were incorporated into the regular season fixtures, with clubs playing home and away matches against all the other sides on their side of the Pennines. The fixture structure in what was one division of all the professional clubs – apart from two seasons in the 1960s – did not see home and away games against all the opponents in the Northern Rugby Football League, except for those internecine derby clashes within the county confines in what was, effectively, a series of battles within the war. Leeds had the best record in the Yorkshire League Championship, winning it on 14 occasions and being runners-up a further 8 times. Their nearest challengers were Huddersfield, who were the only other side to get into double figures, winning the trophy on 11 occasions and finishing second a further 10 times. The Loiners finished second four times, in 1914/15 (to Huddersfield), 1918/19 (to Hull), 1924/5 (to Hull K.R.) and 1926/7 (to Hull) before their inaugural triumph in 1927/8 when they ended ahead of Featherstone. The blue and ambers retained the tag for the first time in 1934/5, claiming top spot five times in the 1930s, a feat they matched in the 1960s, being the four-time holders when the competition was scrapped.

Leeds' Yorkshire League triumphs

Yorkshire Senior Competition
1901/2 – finished 9 points ahead of Manningham
Yorkshire League Championship
1927/8 – finished 7 points ahead of Featherstone Rovers
1930/1 – finished 2 points ahead of Huddersfield
1933/4 – finished 1 point ahead of Hunslet
1934/5 – finished 6 points ahead of Hull
1936/7 – finished 3 points ahead of Castleford
1937/8 – finished 1 point ahead of Hunslet
1950/1 – finished 6 points ahead of Halifax

1954/5 – finished 4 points ahead of Halifax
1956/7 – finished 1 point ahead of Hull
1960/1 – finished 8 points ahead of Wakefield
1966/7 – finished 2 points ahead of Hull K.R.
1967/8 – finished 9 points ahead of Hull K.R.
1968/9 – finished 13 points ahead of Castleford
1969/70 – finished 9 points ahead of Castleford

THEY SAID IT

'When the name Arthur Clues crops up in conversation, eyes light up or brows furrow, for he is the stuff of which memories are made. Tall tales are told about Arthur and many of them are true. In short, he was both beguiling and brutal, riveting and ruthless.'

Rugby League historian Robert Gate's appreciation of one of Leeds' finest exponents

FIVE HEADINGLEY REP GAMES

On five occasions, 'exhibition' internationals have been played at Headingley Carnegie Stadium:

6 May 1935 – British RL 25 France 18
19 May 1951 – Great Britain 20 Australasia 23
16 April 1958 – British RL XIII 19 France 8
6 November 1966 – Rest of the League 38 GB Tourists 31
29 October 1988 – Whitbread Trophy Challenge – Great Britain 30 Rest of the World 28

To coincide with the opening of the ultimately ill-fated Whitbread Hall of Fame at the Bentley Arms in Oulton, a match was staged between the home nation and the rest of the world. A crowd of almost 12,500 saw Great Britain triumph against the visitors who included players from Australia, New Zealand, Papua New Guinea and France. Wally Lewis was supposed to have led the ROW outfit but broke his arm in the World Cup final, Kiwi Mark Graham taking over. Leeds provided four players for the home side, centres and try-scorers Garry Schofield and David Stephenson, who kicked five goals, and forwards Hugh Waddell and Roy Powell. In the World XIII ranks, prop 'Slammin' Sam Backo was on a season secondment to Leeds and Cliff Lyons was in his second spell here.

EUROPE'S BEST, WORLD'S FINEST

Twenty-six years before Leeds were crowned World Club Champions for the first time when beating Canterbury, they conquered Europe. As defending champions, a one-off match was arranged at Headingley in front of a creditable 5,145 fans against their French counterparts, principally for television and the testing of colour pictures. Leeds romped to a 31–5 success against a side that had won the French domestic double as XIII Catalan, the forerunners of the current Catalans Dragons. John Atkinson led the way with four of his side's nine tries but the French were spared further embarrassment as Leeds kicked only two goals.

On two occasions Leeds have been crowned the best team on the planet with thrilling victories at Elland Road. In 2005, a majestic first-half performance was the platform for a thrilling 39–32 success over the Bulldogs while three years later Melbourne were grounded in a storm 11–4, Kevin Sinfield dropping crucial goals in both matches. Manly redressed the balance for the NRL in 2009, when they won 28–20 at the same venue.

THEY SAID IT

'Gary, I know you will be successful – but not tonight, old friend. Tonight you are going to get your bum kicked.'

Sheffield coach Phil Larder's unfortunate message to Leeds Chief Executive Gary Hetherington – prior to his side losing 30–18 in Super League II

CHRISTMAS PRESENT

The Christmas period traditionally saw a hectic series of matches, most of them passionate local derbies, where there was little neighbourly cheer. The schedule for part-time players was invariably three games in four days and four in a week and, on two occasions, matches were played on three consecutive afternoons. Until 1959, when they lost 8–6 at Batley's Mount Pleasant, Leeds more often than not played on Christmas Day, a huge public holiday for the working support until the Boxing Day game became more firmly established as the highlight of the festive programme. The 'Gallant Youths' have provided the opposition on the most occasions, 25 out of the 44 matches Leeds have played on the holy day and although the blue and ambers hold the upper hand overall, early on they could not buy a point let alone a win against them. Batley won the first five clashes, between 1909 and 1914, the Loiners not scoring in four of them. There have been two Christmas Day draws, both at Headingley against Batley (1916) and Wakefield (1937), bizarrely both 0–0. Leeds' biggest win on Christmas Day was over Batley in 1954 when Drew Turnbull scored four tries and fellow winger George Broughton a hat-trick in a 50–6 success and Bramley had the misfortune of being easily beaten on all four occasions they were the opposition. Only once have Leeds played a team from across the border when

Oldham were beaten in 1942. The most famous Christmas Day encounter was in 1908 when a crowd of over 12,000 witnessed a thrilling game against the inaugural Kangaroo tourists. The Aussies raced into an early lead thanks to a brace of tries and a goal by outstanding North Sydney centre Jim Devereux who later signed for Hull and was in their side defeated by Leeds in the 1910 Challenge Cup final replay. Winger Ernie Oliver, who had been signed in March from Northampton RU, replied in the corner for Leeds, Frank Young converting before Walsh for the tourists and Ward swapped tries to make it 11–8 to the visitors at the break. Young kicked a penalty to narrow the gap but a forward rush saw Green and Golds hooker Sandy Pearce go over. With the crowd getting increasingly animated, Leeds attacked relentlessly in the final quarter of the match and had four tries disallowed, leaving the Australians 14–10 victors. Notoriously, in 1925 the Christmas Day match away at Batley which was lost 10–5 had to be replayed when it was discovered that the pitch had not been properly marked out. Batley won the second clash 5–0 in mid-March.

Leeds on Christmas Day

	Played	Won	Lost	Drawn
Liversedge	1	0	1	0
Manningham	1	1	0	0
Bradford	3	1	2	0
Batley	25	16	8	1
Hunslet	3	1	2	0
Bramley	4	4	0	0
Dewsbury	1	1	0	0
Wakefield	4	2	1	1
Oldham	1	1	0	0
Featherstone	1	0	1	0
Australia	1	0	1	0

THEY SAID IT

'That's the best £500 worth of free publicity Leeds have ever spent.'

Sky Sports front man Eddie Hemmings commenting on Ronnie the Rhino's 1997 election campaign!

BIG WINS & A DRAW

On two occasions, Leeds have topped the century in matches, one in the League and the other the Challenge Cup. Against ailing Coventry in the final match of the 1912/13 season, Loiners posted two club records; Fred Webster crossing for 8 tries and every player getting their name on the score sheet among 24 touchdowns in a 102–0 success. That stood as Leeds' biggest win until they faced Second Division Swinton at Gigg Lane in a fourth round cup tie in February 2001. The Rhinos raced in for 19 tries against Mike Gregory's beleaguered men, Iestyn Harris leading the way with 38 points from a try and 17 goals while imports Brett Mullins with two, Bradley Clyde and Robbie Mears all scored on their debuts. The highest score Leeds have posted in a First Division game was their 90–0 shellacking of Barrow in February 1990, seven players each scoring two tries. Leeds were also involved in the highest ever draw when they shared 92 points with Sheffield Eagles at Headingley Carnegie in April 1994, teenagers Francis Cummins with two tries and Graham Holroyd, who scored 18 points from a try and seven goals, among their scorers.

JUNIOR INTERNATIONALS

Following a reorganisation of international competition in 1976, the Great Britain Under-24s were introduced on a regular basis, having previously played four matches in the 1960s. From 1984, the age limit was changed and lowered by three years.

Great Britain Under-24s – 1976–83 (3 players)
Roy Dickinson (prop) – 5 caps 1976-8; 4 v France, 1 v Australia
David Smith (winger) – 2 caps 1976 v France
David Ward (hooker) – 2 caps 1976 v France

Great Britain Under-21s – 1984–95 (15 players)
Paul Anderson (prop) – 2 caps 1992-3 v France
Mark Conway (scrum-half) – 1 cap 1984 v France
David Creasser (centre) – 5 caps 1984-6; 4 v France, 1 v New Zealand
Francis Cummins (winger) – 2 caps 1984-5; 1 v Australia, 1 v France
Paul Delaney (half-back) – 2 caps 1991 v France
Vince Fawcett (winger) – 3 caps 1990-1 v France
Bobbie Goulding (scrum-half) – 1 cap 1991 v Papua New Guinea
Brendan Hill (prop) – 1 cap 1986 v France
Graham Holroyd (stand-off) – 1 cap 1993 v France
Errol Johnson (centre) – 2 caps 1988 v France
Jim Leatham (prop) – 1 cap 1994 v France
Paul Medley (second-row) – 2 caps 1987 v France
Roy Powell (second-row) – 5 caps 1984-6; 4 v France, 1 v New Zealand
Richard Pratt (winger) – 2 caps 1988 v France
Gareth Stephens (scrum-half) – 3 caps 1993; 2 v France, 1 v New Zealand

In 1991/2 the RFL modified the junior set-up, with the institution of a Great Britain Academy representative side, building on the earlier work of the GB Colts. The Academy was originally for players up to the age of 19 although the limit was dropped to 18. In 1994 the Academy toured Australia, losing their two tests against the Australians 46–8 and 64–10 and winning only one tour match. Francis Cummins, Paul Cook, Graham Holroyd, Carl Pearson and Marcus Vassilakopoulos were selected in the John Kear-coached squad. Hull-born prop Pearson was the only one of the quintet who did not play first-team rugby at Headingley.

In 1996, Ray Unsworth took a tour to New Zealand where the renowned Junior Kiwis won the series 3–0. Leeds provided Gavin Brown, Jamie Field, Nick Fozzard, Marvin Golden, Terry Newton and Marcus St Hilaire with Nathan McAvoy – who was to briefly sign for the Rhinos – the captain. The 2001 Academy tour created history by beating the Kiwis on their own soil for the first time, astonishingly winning 72–16 in the Second Test although both encounters with the Aussies were lost. Mike Gregory was the coach and Rob Burrow skipper, the squad also containing Headingley Carnegie youngsters Dwayne Barker, Richie Mathers, Danny McGuire, Gareth Morton and Jason Netherton in their number. Three years later, an Under-18s Academy side which included John Gallagher, David Doherty and Lee Smith among their scorers ended the Australian Schoolboys' 100 per cent record on home soil. The Joeys had Greg Inglis in their ranks but went down 33–24. The two Tests with the Kiwis were shared. Other Leeds players to play Academy international rugby include Ryan Bailey, Anthony Barrett, Chris Chapman, Garreth Carvell, Darren Hughes, Jamie Jones-Buchanan, Lee Maher, Adrian Morley, Matt Schultz, Kevin Sinfield, Kris Smith and David Wrench.

UNLUCKY BREAK

One of the shortest careers on record at Leeds is that of second-rower Alan Rathbone. At a time when Leeds were reshaping their side in 1987, after near relegation, they twice broke the transfer record as a host of players went through what seemed to be a revolving dressing room door. One of the less heralded and more surprising captures was that of former Leigh, Rochdale and Bradford hard man Rathbone, a man who took no prisoners and arrived, somewhat surprisingly, from Warrington for £32,500 in July. Training well during the off-season and given the vice captaincy, he made his debut against former club Leigh at Headingley in the opening match of the new campaign. Barely a quarter of an hour in, he was back in the dressing room with a badly fractured jaw which it was said would keep him out for three months. He never pulled on the shirt again.

APPEARANCES & DEBUTS

While all records are there to be broken, some remain timeless. It is extremely unlikely, with the reduced length of the season and lesser number of cup competitions now played, that John Holmes' appearance record for the club will ever be surpassed. On debut as a 16-year-old in 1968 – when he posted another club best with 23 points from ten goals and a try against Hunslet in the Lazenby Cup – his 21-year career spanned 625 matches, 604 of them starting appearances and 21 off the bench. That is over 80 more than the next great servant, durable prop Fred Webster who arrived on the eve of his 20th birthday from Brotherton and played for 18 seasons, making 543 starts – which would have been more but for the First World War. He captained the Loiners to their first trophy in 1910, scoring a try in the Challenge Cup final replay against Hull. John Atkinson (518 in total) is the only other Leeds player to wear the colours more than 500 times. Modern gladiator David Ward shares with cultured full-back from the 1930s and '40s Jim Brough the same number of starts, 442, but Ward played a further 40 times off the bench.

With tries worth 4 points rather than 3 when John Holmes made his bow, former Stanningley centre Ashley Gibson nearly matched the best introduction feat, notching 22 points, courtesy of 3 tries and 5 goals at Leigh in 1995. Other players to register a hat-trick on debut are; Marcus Bai (winger v London Broncos, home 2004), Eric Grothe (winger v Leigh, home, January 1985), Cliff Lyons (stand-off v Keighley, home, August 1985, Yorkshire Cup), Bryan Adams (second-row v Salford, away, 1974), David Smith (winger v Bramley, away, 1976, Lazenby Cup). All were scored in big wins apart from that by the only forward in the group, 'Butch' Adams who, astonishingly, was Leeds' only try-scorer in a disastrous 61–13 defeat at the Willows. Winger Alan Smith made the most eye-catching first start, crossing for four touchdowns in an Eastern Division clash at home to Dewsbury in August 1962.

Leeds' youngest ever debutant is scrum-half Barry Seabourne, who was 16 years and 97 days old when facing Hull K.R. in the final game of the 1962/3 season, a 34–11 Craven Park loss.

ONE AND ONLY

Up to the end of the 2009 season, twelve players had pulled on the blue and amber shirt just once in Super League. The latest pair were substitutes Dane Manning and Jay Pitts who have the opportunity to add to that tally after being given squad numbers for 2010. Before them, in 2008, Michael Haley, who moved on to Doncaster, and ex-Churwell Chief Joe

Chandler, were part of a young side that memorably defeated Castleford at Headingley, 18–12, with several first-teamers away on international duty. Of the remaining eight aspirants, for five of them one sip of summer domestic competition was their only taste while at the club. Scott Murrell got his shot at home to Leigh in May 2005, as a substitute, as did Jonny Hepworth two years earlier away in the capital against London Broncos, both drawing winning pay. Stand-off Jon Liddell had more of a baptism of fire, being one of the side's few successes in a heavy defeat at Wigan in early 2001 while Chris Chapman's only exploit was off the bench against Hull two years earlier. Perhaps the unluckiest was Kiwi Nathan Picchi who came from Hawkes Bay Unicorns and was instrumental in Leeds achieving their first ever Super League victory, against Sheffield, at Headingley in round five of the inaugural season in 1996. He replaced Mike Forshaw but lasted just over 50 minutes before being forced from the fray with a badly damaged shoulder, never to reappear. The same injury afflicted centre Paul Bell in 2000, his only championship appearance coming against Wakefield in a home loss although he did play in three Challenge Cup ties prior to returning home to Australia. Namesake Dean heroically came out of retirement to don the shirt against Paris in late 1996, his try spurring the side to a victory that effectively staved off the threat of relegation. It was the then coach's only venture onto the field in the summer and came some 12 years after his 22 other appearances for the club. Prop Jim Leatham also made one Super League entrance, off the bench alongside debutant Iestyn Harris in a one point home defeat against Wigan in 1997, his other nine matches coming under Doug Laughton in the winter and he subsequently moved on to Hull. Garry Schofield actually made one start for Leeds when the code switched seasons but that was in the Challenge Cup in 1996 when the Loiners just scraped home at lowly Swinton.

MATCHES OFF

The Rhinos' thrilling success over St Helens at Old Trafford to take the 2009 title was the 2,376th Super League encounter. In the 14 seasons since the revolutionary change, only six matches have been postponed and two of those have been at Headingley Carnegie Stadium. Despite the switch of seasons, a late winter or early spring start means that the vagaries of the British weather can still have an impact, not least on the first weekend in March. Not surprisingly, perhaps, the first clash to miss its original slot on that date was at Bradford – but not at their cavernous, weather-afflicted Odsal bowl home. The game to open the 2001 season between the Bulls and St Helens was staged at Valley Parade where they were temporary tenants and was put back by a day because of snow on the terraces. In March 2002, Leeds' opening Super League fixture at home to London Broncos was delayed from the Friday night to Sunday afternoon following high winds which damaged the North Stand roof. Four years later, again on that date, a patch of frozen ground in front of the South Stand caused the encounter with Castleford to be similarly rearranged. June flooding in Hull meant that their encounter with Salford in round 18 in 2007 was played a month later and, in 2008, Wigan put back their mid-summer game with Huddersfield owing to their JJB Stadium pitch needing reseeding. All the host sides won on the new dates with the exception of the Warriors. The start of the 2009 season saw the sixth call off when Harlequins' pitch at the Stoop was frozen over and their match against Bradford was called off. The game had originally been scheduled to be played on 22 February but was brought forward by a week – and subsequently put back to August – to accommodate Quins playing Australian side Manly, as a warm up for the Sea Eagles' World Club Challenge encounter with Leeds.

ALL SQUARE

The most number of draws Leeds have accrued in a championship season is five, in 1903/4, when they played 37 fixtures in total. Matches with cup holders Halifax away and Broughton Rangers at home both ended in a pointless stalemate; trips across the Pennines to Oldham and Wigan saw 4 points shared and the clash with Leigh at Headingley finished 3–3, as the Loiners ended up fifth in the overall standings.

Their first ever draw, in their ninth match of the inaugural Northern Union fixtures in 1895/6, was a similar scoreline and came in the home derby with Hunslet, while in December that season there were consecutive 0–0 thrillers with Bradford and Tyldesley; the latter the fourth consecutive match in which Leeds did not concede a point. The first season without a drawn game was 1911/12 and they became virtually non-existent for most of the 1950s and '60s.

In the penultimate league match of the 1954/5 campaign, on 11 April, Leeds drew 13–13 at Wheldon Road, Castleford; Lewis Jones claiming all their points. They shared 50 with Salford in October 1957 and suffered a surprise holding to 9–9 at Batley in an Eastern Division game in August 1962. Their next one-point encounter came at Belle Vue in September 1968, ending a run of almost six complete seasons without a draw, the longest period in the club's history.

The Super League summer that contained the most drawn matches for the Rhinos was 2003 and all of them were at home, twice with Wigan – which both finished 24–24 – and a 10–10 deadlock with Hull.

ICON OF A GENERATION 4 – ARTHUR CLUES

Leeds have signed some of the greatest Australian talent over the decades but few have had a bigger impact than gregarious Arthur Clues. His impending arrival in 1947 galvanised the city as the club unveiled an ex-policeman who had grown up, and held his own, in the tough suburbs of western Sydney. 'Big A' arrived with a reputation, he was not so much famous as notorious, having been sent off in a Test match against the touring Great Britain 'Indomitables' during the 1946 series at the Sydney Cricket Ground. He made his eagerly awaited debut alongside Kiwi Bert Cook on 1 February at home to Hull and even though the Loiners were narrowly defeated, a star was born who many rated as the finest second-rower ever to grace the colours. Renowned for his physically intimidating presence, the post-war hero was also a magnificent broken field runner, possessed a wonderful array of kicks and had a delicate side step for such a big man. He led from the front, eventually taking on the captaincy but was thwarted in his quest for major honours, not least at Wembley in 1947, Leeds having made the decider without conceding a point but going down to Bradford. In 1949/50, he was joint top try-scorer with 16 but Warrington ended his Challenge Cup ambitions this time, in the semi-final at Odsal. Magnificent for fostering team spirit, he took on the club's directors with as much passion and disregard as he did opponents and it was no surprise – but a massive disappointment – when he transferred to neighbours Hunslet. A measure of the impact made and esteem with which he was held was seen when he returned to Headingley for the first time on Good Friday 1955 and attracted an astonishing 23,000 crowd. A cricket lover, he played for Bill Fallowfield's side that raised thousands of pounds for charity and became the Aussie who never went home. A larger than life character, he and Leeds were synonymous; his famous sports shop ensuring that junior sides got properly kitted out – invariably at his own expense. In his later years he was a very valuable, long-serving member of the Sports Council and its Sports Aid Foundation and was captain at Moortown golf club. Stories abound about him and he was a fantastic self-propagandist but he remains the only player to have scored a try and a century at both Headingley and the Sydney Cricket ground.

INVERTED NAMES

With only a hint of artistic licence, a Leeds side made up of players whose surnames could have been their first names includes a winger from the current Rhinos squad:

1 Paul Gill
2 Scott Donald
3 Tony Carroll
4 Wally Desmond
5 Len Kenny
6 Dicky Ralph
7 Les Adams
8 Harvey Howard
9 Graham Joyce
10 Shaun Wane
11 Bill Ramsey
12 Jimmy Douglas
13 Iowerth Isaac

Substitutes

14 Abe Terry
15 Danny Allan
16 Niel James
17 Alan Julian

The coach, of course, would have to be Roy Francis.

EARLIEST START, LATEST FINISH

Super League XIII represented the earliest beginning to a summer campaign for the Rhinos, when they faced Hull K.R. at Headingley on 2 February – although that will be broken when they travel to Wrexham to launch the 2010 season at the Crusaders on Friday 29 January. [QUERY]That 2008 start was almost exactly two months ahead of their first ever summer clash against Warrington – which was on 31 March 1996. It even pre-dated the Challenge Cup ties that used to take place prior to the start of the championship season, before the closing rounds of that competition were moved to later in the year.

Pre-Super League, when the sport was played in winter, the first time the domestic season went into May was in 1918/19 when the Emergency League that had operated during the First World War ran until mid-January, before normal competition was resumed. The final championship fixture that season was played on 10 May at Hull K.R., a week after the Lazenby Cup clash with Hunslet which, until 1926, was the traditional season climax rather than opener.

Not surprisingly, perhaps, the latest ever finish to a league campaign came after the big freeze of 1963. Headingley was unable to stage a match for four months from the start of December, the team playing only five away fixtures in that time, and the side ended up facing 18 matches in 55 days; including on the 10th, 12th, 13th and 15th of April and the 4th, 6th and 8th of May. The final round, again at Hull K.R., was on 24 May, the same date that Leeds won the Championship final six years later. The latest play-off finish came 10 years after that when Bradford were thrashed at Fartown in the 1979 Premiership decider which, after another long, harsh winter, was staged on 27 May.

RHINOS AT THE MOVIES

A Leeds team to watch at the cinema, by position:

1 Brent *Webb of Deceit*
2 *Alias* Alan *Smith and* Lewis *Jones*
3 *The Good, the bad and the Uglee* Smith
4 *E.T.* (Andrew Ettingshausen)
5 *Annie* Ryan *Hall*
6 Danny *Jerry Mcguire*
7 Barry *Seabourne Identity*
8 *Saving Private Ryan* Bailey
9 Mick *Shawshank Redemption*
10 *Singing in the* Keith *Rayne*
11 *Snow* Brendan *White and the Seven Dwarfs*
12 *Indiana* Jamie *Jones*-Buchanan
13 *Bonnie and* Bradley *Clyde*

Substitutes

14 *Cool Hand Luke* Burgess
15 *Ben Hur* Jones-Bishop
16 *Free Willie* Poching
17 *Man with the Golden* Richard *Gunn*

Coach – *Life of Brian* McClennan
Manager – *Arthur* Clues
Timekeeping – *Billy* Watts *Elliot*

In readiness for a game against Manly *Where* Sea *Eagles Dare* Starring, Ian *Kirke Douglas*, Greg *Clint Eastwood* and Scott *Donald Sutherland.*

FIRST DEFEATS

The first team to beat Leeds after the switch to Northern Union were Widnes, in the second game of the 1895/6 season, the Chemics triumphing 11–8 at Lowerhouse Lane. Stand-off J. Bastow, in his only season for the Loiners after the breakaway, scored one of their two tries and added a goal. Initial lowering of the colours by a Yorkshire team came five matches later when Wakefield Trinity were victorious 8–3 at Belle Vue. A week before that, Stockport became the first side to win at Headingley, one of only four matches staged between the clubs, the honours of which were shared overall. Leeds gained a measure of revenge over the men from Cheshire in their only other Headingley meeting, in February 1903, winning 30–0 with Welsh wonder winger W. Evans crossing for a club record 5 tries in a match on his way to another landmark of 28 touchdowns in a season.

Leeds' first loss in a cup tie came in the second round of the Northern Union Cup in its inaugural campaign of 1896/7, when they went down 9–3 at Tyldesley, who themselves went out to eventual runners up St Helens in the quarter-final. The name of the premier knockout competition was changed to the Rugby League Challenge Cup in 1923, the year that Leeds beat Hull in the final but their seven match unbeaten run under the new banner was ended in the second round the following season when Wakefield reigned supreme at Headingley, 6–0. Leeds had little good fortune in the early years of the Yorkshire Cup, their participation ended first time out in 1905 when – despite a try by former Broughton Ranger J.W. Stead – they were defeated 7–5 at home to Halifax.

The ill-fated Captain Morgan Trophy for the first round winners in the county cups, which lasted a single season in 1973/4, saw Leeds' hopes ended in the semi-final by subsequent winners Warrington, at Headingley. Five years later the John Player Trophy was instituted as a winter filler for television,

Leeds again not getting past the opening round at the first time of asking, St Helens dashing their hopes 16–11 at Knowsley Road, despite the sides sharing six tries. Saints were also the first team to defeat the Loiners in a Floodlit Trophy clash, in a qualifying game in 1965/6, on the competition's initiation. Leeds entered the Championship play-offs for the first time in 1914/15 and, having beaten Wigan at Central Park to make the decider, were thrashed 35–2 by the Huddersfield 'Team of all the Talents' for whom legends Harold Wagstaff, Doug Clark and Ben Gronow, with a brace, were among their try-scorers. When that competition was revamped as the Premiership in the mid-1970s, Leeds were defending champions when they lost both semi-final legs to St Helens in 1975/6.

LEEDS FOODIES

A blue and amber selection made up of the finest produce or from purveyors of sustenance:

Alan Tait and Lyle
Jim Bacon
Les Dyl
Robin Dewhurst's the butchers
Mark Campbell's soups
Syd Hynes
Craig Coleman's mustard
Steve Pickles
Tony Currie
Harold Rowe
Jimmy 'Colonel' Sanders
Graham Eccles cake
Cliff Lyons
Chev Walker's crisps
W.N. Whiting

THEY SAID IT

'People said that I feigned injury and that I winked when I was on the stretcher. Well, I can honestly say that I might have blinked but I didn't wink! I really did take a knock and woke up in the dressing room being attended to by the Wembley doctor.'

Alex Murphy on his 1971 Wembley clash with Syd Hynes that saw the Leeds centre become the first player to be dismissed at the Twin Towers

RHINOS IN THE PLAY-OFFS

Excluding their six Grand Final appearances, the Rhinos have appeared in the summer play-offs on 22 occasions to date, against 9 different opponents. Results have been mixed with 10 victories and a dozen heart-wrenching defeats. Halifax were Leeds' first opponents, the only time the then Blue Sox made the post-season and they were downed at Headingley in 1998. Conversely, Warrington's sole visit brought them the narrowest of victories with a last-gasp Lee Briers drop goal haunting the blue and amber fans but providing an iconic televisual moment. Castleford have visited the Leeds bastion twice in consecutive seasons with the Rhinos gaining revenge for defeat in Graham Murray's last match in charge and Hull have been overcome at home in their sole meeting, much to the black and white's chagrin. The Rhinos had to learn how to win against Wigan, the code's big-hitters having come together on six occasions, the Warriors winning the first three clashes until momentum swung the other way. Swords have also been crossed with Saints half a dozen times with the Merseysiders holding sway overall. Leeds' nemesis has been Bradford, losing out to the Bulls on all three occasions that the derby rivals have met on the road to Old Trafford. It took until the Rhinos' 15th play-off game before they won away, at Knowsley Road in 2005, which remains their only travelling success. In 2009, two new names were added to the list as Hull K.R. and then Catalans were vanquished.

Record

	P	W	L	F	A
Halifax	1	1	0	13	6
Wigan	6	3	3	138	117
St Helens	6	2	4	125	156
Castleford	2	1	1	38	37
Bradford	3	0	3	38	102
Hull	1	1	0	36	22
Warrington	1	0	1	16	17
Hull K.R.	1	1	0	44	8
Catalans	1	1	0	27	20
Total	22	10	12	475	485
Home	13	9	4		
Away	9	1	8		

WHAT'S IN A NAME?

The surname to have graced the blue and amber shirt the most since the formation of the Northern Union is Davies. Starting with forward B. Davies, who made his debut in the opening day win over Holbeck to launch the 1896 season and went on to appear 71 times, ten different Davies derivatives have represented the club. The last was Welshman John, the Union international from Neath who arrived in

1964, not long before ex-Bradford stand-off Derek Davies moved on to Hull. The most famous and longest-serving Davieses played together, W.H. and W.A. arriving from the Principality within four months of each other in 1912/13. 'Hughie' was a prolific winger from Nantyglo who scored 117 tries in 179 appearances and twice set records for the number of touchdowns in a season for the club. Centre 'Willie' was at Headingley for 12 glorious seasons, featuring in the famous 1914 'Rorke's Drift' Test win in Sydney and was behind only Fred Harrison and Billy Ward when he retired, after playing 278 times for the Loiners. He kicked a goal in Leeds' first Yorkshire Cup triumph, over Dewsbury at Halifax in 1921. Nine Smiths have graced the colours with many of them being wingers – Stan, Alan, David, Andy and Lee. Tied in third, David's son Danny Ward was the eighth of his line, and there have been the same number of Joneses although that total excludes Jamie Jones-Buchanan and Ben Jones-Bishop. Chev and Ben Walker took their surname's representation to seven and, completing the top five, there have been six Thomases and a similar number of Evanses around the place.

INTERNATIONAL FORTRESS HEADINGLEY

Thirty-one Test matches have taken place on the rugby side of the world's only dual Test arena, with the national team beating the tourists on 25 occasions. The ground staged the first ever such encounter when the Northern Union defeated A.H. Baskiville's New Zealand 'All Golds' 14–6 in front of 8,182 fans on 25 January 1908. The Kiwis were the first to break the Headingley hoodoo for representative sides in 1955, at the eleventh time of asking, Tommy Baxter's side winning 28–13 in the Third Test although they had already lost the series; Leeds' Lewis Jones and Gordon Brown were among Great Britain's try-scorers. It took the Kangaroos until 1973 to record a win at the Leeds headquarters, their tenth attempt, Graham 'Wombat' Eadie's five goals proving to be the key in a 14–6 success.

On three previous occasions, including the first time the Green and Golds had taken to the turf in a Test at Headingley, they had agonisingly gone down by a point. In October 1921, Leeds winger Squire Stockwell's try proved to be the difference in a 6–5 success in front of a British record attendance of 32,000 fans. In 1937, a similar number saw Emlyn Jenkins' try split the sides 5–4 and in 1959 Johnny Whiteley's touchdown in the Second Test secured an 11–10 victory, the last time Great Britain held the Ashes on home soil. That match also saw arguably the fastest try scored in a Test when Leeds prop Don Robinson crossed at the end of the first move of the game following a charge down. The Kiwis also lost by the same odd point in 21 in 1947, but they became the first nation to win twice at Headingley and by a then record margin in the opening Test of the 1961 series. They were victorious 29–11, full-back Jack Fagan kicking seven goals for Don Hammond's men, the captain claiming one of his side's five tries.

Great Britain's biggest defeat at Headingley came in 1982 courtesy of Max Krilich's all-conquering Kangaroo 'Invincibles', the skipper again on the score sheet. However, Steve Evans did have the consolation of crossing for the only try against them over the three Test series, in the old dressing room corner.

The French have taken some fearful beatings on their ten visits, the last eight of which have been the only Test matches played at Headingley since 1984. Martin Offiah set a record when he went over five times against the Tricolores in 1991 and Great Britain ran in 13 tries two years later in a record 72–6 dismantling. France's sole success came in April 1990 when they ran out 25–18 victors, David Fraisse's goals and two drop goals from Gilles Dumas proving to be the difference. In 1959 and 1993 the ground staged two Tests – against the French in spring and the respective touring Antipodeans in late autumn.

Great Britain Record at Headingley:

	P	W	L	F	A
Australia	12	9	3	132	139
New Zealand	9	7	2	148	117
France	10	9	1	429	96
Total	31	25	6	709	352

THEY SAID IT

'Nay Dennis, we're not having any of that are we?'

Leeds skipper Mick Clark's question to Dennis Hartley during a Challenge Cup tie against Castleford in the late 1960s, after he had been punched in the face as the teams packed down for the first scrum.

'Yes lad we are, all bloody eighty minutes of it,'

is reported to have been Dennis's reply.

ICON OF A GENERATION 5 – ERIC HARRIS

Eric Harris was Leeds Rugby's first superstar. Unknown and unheralded when he arrived from the Queensland country, he went on to smash every try-scoring record in a glittering nine years at the club. In an era when prolific wingers were the norm, he helped give Leeds a cutting edge and was at the heart of their first golden era throughout the 1930s. Recruited by centre partner Jeff Moores, whom he played with at Brisbane Wests, he immediately earned the nickname 'Toowoomba Ghost' for his ability to accelerate away from despairing defenders who thought they had his measure. In 383 appearances, ended at the outbreak of the Second World War, he scored just over a try a game (392), beginning with two on his debut against Featherstone. That announced the arrival of a supreme finisher who rapidly became a huge draw card, the Headingley faithful thrilling to his blistering touchline dashes, poise and balance. His presence in 1930 sparked a 17-match unbeaten run which included the capture of the Yorkshire Cup, when he crossed for the game-breaking try against Huddersfield. It was the start of him grabbing the big game scores. By the end of his first season he had registered 58 touchdowns, almost double the previous Leeds best. He posted the only try in the 1932 Challenge Cup final as Swinton were beaten at Wigan, beating two despairing cover defenders on a glory charge that covered over half the length of the pitch. Moores was replaced by Fred Harris from Leigh which saw another glorious partnership emerge, not least when the pair perfected a dummy scissors trademark move. In 1935/6 Eric Harris had his best return, with a club record 63 tries – that still stands. It included seven in a game at Acton, creating and scoring a glorious touchdown at Wembley and going over the whitewash in a Rugby League record 17 consecutive matches from December to March, which yielded 36 tries. Among his other landmarks, he equalled the club record of 8 tries in a match against Bradford in September 1931, scored a record 9 hat-tricks in a season in 1930/1 and 1935/6 and is the quickest Leeds player to a century of tries, achieved in 91 games. With 42 hat-tricks in his Leeds career, he is on exactly double the next contender. One of his most important touchdowns came in the Championship semi-final at Headingley against Swinton when his long-range interception ensured an 'All Leeds' decider against Hunslet. On his return home he donned the maroon of Queensland against New South Wales in 1940, the Second World War preventing him winning a Test cap.

TOP TEN SUPER LEAGUE COMEBACKS

Some successes are fashioned on the back of seemingly certain defeat which makes the taste of victory that much more satisfying. Here are ten such summer occasions when the sour became sweet.

1) Wakefield 30 Leeds 32 – 10 July 2009
At 14 points ahead on the hour, it seemed certain that the Wildcats were going to register their first home Super League win against their derby rivals. Although Ali Lauitiiti narrowed the gap, Leeds were a man down in the closing stages – with Brent Webb sin-binned – but still produced the ultimate smash-and-grab raid. With two minutes remaining Rob Burrow crossed to set up the astonishing denouement, Carl Ablett collecting Danny McGuire's grubber and the stand-off being alive again in the move and showing great presence despite stumbling to send Scott Donald across in the corner on the last play.

2) Leeds 42 Bradford 38 – Millennium Magic, Cardiff, 6 May 2007
A wondrous win at the death amid huge controversy, as Jordan Tansey raced onto Kevin Sinfield's penalty from out wide, which came back off the post, to steal the points. For the administrators who had taken the bold decision to stage a round of matches as a stand-alone event, the perfect finish to generate the column

inches, especially as video replays confirmed that the last-gasp penalty should not have been given and the poacher was offside. Not that the jubilant Rhinos fans were bothered, especially at the sight of their crestfallen, indignant rivals.

3)Leeds 30 St Helens 20 – 12 September 2003

At 20 points down with 63 minutes gone, the Rhinos staged an astonishing fightback to grab the spoils. Rob Burrow's try began the revival immediately followed by a Mark Calderwood score. With the noise levels rising, Gary Connolly and Richie Mathers crossed in consecutive sets, Kevin Sinfield on target with all the conversions and to gild the blitz. Then Willie Poching went over in the final minute of a breathless closing quarter.

4) London Broncos 18 Leeds 50 – 3 March 2001

The opening match of the season in the biting cold of the Valley and within 20 minutes the men from the capital were almost as many points up, after tries to Steele Retchless, Jason Hetherington and Shane Millard. Only a desperate cover tackle by Karl Pratt on Denis Moran prevented further damage, the Broncos playmaker being helped off injured as Chev Walker crossed for the first of what were to be 9 Rhinos tries and a subsequent point-a-minute blitz; Keith Senior leading the way with a hat-trick.

5) Sheffield Eagles 23 Leeds 24 – 23 May 1998

Just before the hour at Don Valley Stadium unbeaten Leeds were out of it, 23–4 down and reduced to 12 men with the sending off of Adrian Morley for a high tackle on former Loiner Marcus Vassilakopoulos. Deciding to move the ball wherever possible, wingers Paul Sterling and Francis Cummins sped over, followed by Graham Holroyd to bring the visitors to within a point with 4 minutes left. In the closing seconds the Rhinos were awarded a penalty just inside their own half, referee Stuart Cummins then adding a further 10 metres for supposed dissent by Paul Broadbent. Iestyn Harris duly played the get-out-of-jail card.

6) Wigan Warriors 16 Leeds 24 – 17 February 2006
16 points down at the break, Kevin Sinfield's men produced a gritty second-half reversal to seal the points 2 minutes from time with a Rob Burrow try. Joel Tomkins and Wayne Godwin had come off the bench to score for the hosts, full-back Chris Ashton adding to the Rhinos' misery just before the break. With Jamie Peacock colossal after the interval, Shane Millard and Danny McGuire nipped in for two tries in 4 minutes and Sinfield converted his own touchdown with 6 minutes to go to wrest the lead for the first time and deflate Ian Millward's men.

7) Leeds 38 Hull FC 22 – 6 June 2008
Scott Donald conjured one of the great Headingley Carnegie tries to begin a second half counter-offensive that grabbed the points. Brushing off six players in a wonderful charge for the corner, the winger's effort – straight after Rob Burrow had crossed – eradicated a deficit that had been 20–4 just after half time, Danny Tickle contributing 14 points for the visitors. Inspired by the Aussie wing-man's solo heroics, Gareth Ellis crossed twice and Donald and Burrow both added another for Leeds to complete an ultimately convincing win.

8) Leeds 24 Warrington 22 – 1 August 2009
Lightning does strike twice, and after scuppering Wakefield three weeks earlier, Leeds did it again, sealing victory with the final action. This time it was a conversion, from skipper Kevin Sinfield far out on the South Stand touchline, after he had sent in Scott Donald for the equalising try in the corner with a long pass. Warrington – on Tony Smith's return to his happy Headingley hunting ground – had led throughout, former Rhino Richie Mathers opening the scoring but his ex-team-mates saved the best until last.

9) Castleford 18 Leeds 20 – 31 May 2000

Rebuilding after a horrific start to the campaign and Challenge Cup final loss, Dean Lance's men began a 13-match winning run including two come-from-behind raids. First, Wigan were seen off at home 26–19 after the Warriors had led 19–6 after 55 minutes and then the following midweek, in a game moved because of the Murrayfield decider, the Tigers were clawed back from a similar point in the game after they led 18–6. Keith Senior and Brad Mackay got the Rhinos to within striking distance at the Jungle in front of a record Super League crowd there. In the final minute of a thrilling clash, Ryan Sheridan raced through a gap and Iestyn Harris's conversion sealed matters.

10) Gateshead Thunder 18 Leeds 30 – 22 August 1999

A blitz of 22 points without reply in the second half saw Graham Murray's men stage a Sunday night escape act at the Thunderdome. Two Matt Daylight tries and one from Steve Collins had seen Shaun McRae's charges sweep into an 18–8 interval lead but, superbly marshalled by Daryl Powell, Anthony Farrell, Leroy Rivett and Ryan Sheridan all found the whitewash for the Rhinos to turn the tide.

THE FIERCEST OF RIVALS

The disbanding of the Leeds Parish Church side at the start of the 1901/2 season was the making of Leeds, eight of their top players seeking to join the Headingley ranks including George Mosley – who was later appointed captain – and Jim Birch, who went on to make 232 appearances for the Loiners. The Church side were among the most feared in the game, renowned for their overtly physical approach and vociferous, intimidating fans. When the Clarence Road outfit reached the Northern Union

Cup semi-final in 1900, their drawn home quarter-final with Runcorn attracted 20,000 spectators, such was their pull. In four out of the five seasons the clubs came across each other they finished above Leeds, the ultimate derby rivals meeting eleven times in all, Leeds winning only once across the city in the first ever clash, 3–0, thanks to a Walton penalty.

Complete record v Leeds Parish Church (all league matches)

	P	W	L	D	F	A
Home	5	3	2	0	39	28
Away	6	1	4	1	8	24
Total	11	4	6	1	47	52

LEEDS COUNTRY-SIDE

A 17-man squad made up of Leeds links to nature:

Bernard Poole
J.W. Birch
Joe Busch
Andy Hay
Alf Wood
Jamie Field
Keith Rayne
Gary Moorby
Brendan Hill
F.W. Orchard
W.E. Brook
Vic Hey
F. Mudd
Rob Burrow
Willie Poching
Richard Gunn
Gary Rose

ONE-CAP WONDERS

When he won his ill-fated cap in the Tri-Nations clash with New Zealand at the KC Stadium in November 2004, Matt Diskin became the twenty-fourth Leeds player to be selected for Great Britain once. With the composite side of the islands unlikely to be playing again in the foreseeable future, he joined some of the most famous names to have played for Leeds but who have only pulled on the red, white and blue a single time. Matt's contribution was cut short by severe knee ligament damage after 17 minutes and another Rhino came off the bench for his only appearance in that same game, prop Danny Ward. Two Loiners, expensive centre signing Phil Thomas – who cost £250 when brought from Oldham – and long-serving forward Jim Birch – were the first Test internationals from the club, when they represented the Northern Union in the deciding rubber against the 'All Golds' in Cheltenham in January 1908. The home side lost 8–5 and the pair were not chosen again. Full-back Frank Young played in a Test against the first Kangaroos a year later and although selected for the inaugural tour Down Under in 1910, was injured in the second match and missed the subsequent internationals. Also on that historic trip, Cumbrian second-rower Billy Ward – who was to play over 210 times for Leeds – gained his only honour. On the 1932 tour, scrum-half Les Adams and hooker John Lowe saw action once, the former against Australia and the latter in New Zealand. The Second World War prevented outstanding Welsh prop Dai Prosser from adding to his one cap, gained against Wally Prigg's Aussies in 1937, his compatriot from the Principality Dai Jenkins doing likewise ten years later against the incoming Kiwis, scoring in defeat. Prolific Scottish try machine Drew Turnbull faced the New Zealanders once, four years later in the final Test, crossing twice and hooker Barry Simms faced the French in 1962. Although one of five Leeds backs on the famous 1970 Tour, homesick scrum-half Barry Seabourne only got a chance against New Zealand, while Kevin Rayne emulated twin brother Keith by representing his country, in 1986 in the match with France at Wigan. The ten other one-cappers while with Leeds did win further honours either before they arrived at Headingley, or on leaving. The first, in 1937, was Harry Woods who had initially won his spurs when at Liverpool Stanley. Brian Shaw came into the international arena when with Hunslet, Abe Terry's best days were at St Helens, Lee Crooks debuted when at Hull, Hugh Waddell while with Oldham and current French coach Bobbie Goulding sandwiched his cap at Leeds between ones while at Wigan and Saints. Dick Gemmell, John Bentley, Steve Molloy and Terry Newton were first recognised while wearing the blue and amber but figured again after they had moved on to Hull, Halifax, Featherstone and Wigan respectively.

HOME SWEET HOME

At the completion of the 2009 Super League season, the Rhinos had played 184 regular season matches at Headingley Carnegie Stadium in the competition, excluding play-offs. Of that total, exactly three-quarters have been won but in only one season (2004 when the title was wrested back after 32 years), did the side go through with a perfect record. Ironically, in their first play-off game that year that invincibility was shattered by Bradford. On two other occasions the Bulls have prevented an unbeaten home record, the first under Graham Murray in 1998 and then again five years later, although three matches that year were drawn. The worst season, with seven defeats from eleven fixtures was, not surprisingly, 1996, although in 2001 and again a year later, the famous old ground lost her fortress mantle when six out fourteen fixtures ended in defeat. The highest number of games in a season at home was in 1999 when 15 were scheduled with only Wigan and St Helens returning home with the spoils.

Rhinos Home Records (excluding play-offs)
1996 – won 4 out of 11
1997 – won 8 out of 11
1998 – won 11 out of 12

1999 – won 13 out of 15
2000 – won 9 out of 14
2001 – won 8 out of 14
2002 – won 8 out of 14
2003 – won 10 out of 14
2004 – won 14 out of 14
2005 – won 12 out of 14
2006 – won 10 out of 14
2007 – won 9 out of 13
2008 – won 11 out of 13
2009 – won 11 out of 13

Total – won 138 out of 184

MOST FAMOUS DOG

There was little interest in the opening round clash of the 1978 Challenge Cup when holders Leeds were drawn at home to face a struggling Halifax outfit anchored at the foot of the Second Division. But with frozen weather affecting pitches and the BBC needing a guaranteed fixture to focus upon, the cameras duly arrived on the road to Wembley. Although the visitors put up a gutsy show belying their lowly position, the Loiners won at a canter, scoring seven tries – including doubles for wingers David Smith and John Atkinson – but only kicking two goals and rarely getting into second gear. The inadvertent star of the show though, and a focus of Eddie Waring's commentary became a stray dog who wandered on to the field of play from the South Stand and avoided several efforts to chase it from the hallowed turf. Lingering on the mutt, a producer with the Beeb quickly got his caption writer to flash up the name 'K9', taken from the character in a recently shown *Doctor Who* episode, the dog rather than the game grabbing all the headlines.

LOWEST AGGREGATE

The Rhinos' contentious defeat at Bradford on Good Friday 2009 was their lowest aggregate match score in the regular season of the summer era. The 16-point total in that game was one less than at Wigan and St Helens, seven years apart, which both finished in identical scorelines. On their final appearance at Central Park in 1999, a ground that statistically was the hardest to gain a victory at since the inception of the code, the Rhinos famously took home the spoils 13–4, thanks to tries from Paul Sterling and one – of only three in his Leeds career – for prop Jamie Mathiou. In 2006, on a rain-lashed night at Knowsley Road, Danny Williams claimed the only blue and amber touchdown in a 13–4 defeat. The next two lowest totals both came against Hull, a controversial 10–10 draw in 2003, thanks to the awarding of a late penalty by referee Steve Ganson to the visitors. That came two years after the Rhinos had won 15–6 at another of their historic graveyard venues, the Boulevard; in a match made famous for Danny Ward's shock drop goal, the sole one of his career. The only half of rugby the Rhinos have played that yielded no points was also against Hull, in a riveting clash at the KC Stadium in 2004, the match subsequently finishing in a 23–12 success. The lowest number of points in any game involving Leeds in the Super League era was the 1998 inaugural Grand Final when Wigan were victorious 10–4. In the 2008 World Club Challenge, Leeds were party to their second lowest when Melbourne were defeated 11–4 at Elland Road. Both of those matches were also played in torrential rain.

Top six lowest-scoring Super League regular season games involving Leeds

1 16 – Bradford 10 Leeds 6 – 2009
2 17 – Wigan 4 Leeds 13 – 1999,
St Helens 13 Leeds 4 – 2006

3 20 – Leeds 10 Hull 10 – 2003
4 21 – Hull 6 Leeds 15 – 2001
5 22 – Leeds 14 London 8 – 1999
Leeds 18 Wakefield 4 - 2009
6 24 – Leeds 10 Widnes 14 – 2002,
St Helens 10 Leeds 14 – 2008,
Leeds 10 Wigan 14 – 2008

SELECT BUNCH

A total of three players made their Super League debut for Leeds in 2009, Paul McShane, Dane Manning and Jay Pitts. The year before, seven players made their bows – three of them in the round 19 clash with Castleford, staged on the same weekend as the England v France Test – bringing the total number used by the club since 1996 to 129. A staggering proportion of just over a third of them have played in a Grand Final, with only those who appeared in the first ever decider against Wigan and Andrew Dunemann in 2005, not collecting at least one winner's ring while wearing blue and amber. Two of Graham Murray's boys from 1998 – Iestyn Harris and Adrian Morley – subsequently tasted ultimate victory at Old Trafford, with Bradford against Leeds in 2005, while Jamie Peacock was a three-time winner with the Bulls before he 'came home'. Terry Newton, who also lost with Leeds to the Warriors, was in the cherry and white ranks on three further occasions when they came up short on the last night. David Furner, on the other hand, was a loser with Wigan in 2003 but a winner as a Rhino the following year. A further 'team' of 13 players have donned the Headingley Carnegie colours and also gone on to play in Grand Finals with other clubs; Paul Anderson (Bradford, St Helens), James Lowes (Bradford), Nathan McAvoy (Bradford), Kevin Iro (St Helens), Graham

Mackay (Bradford), Mike Forshaw (Bradford), Gary Connolly (Wigan), Harvey Howard (Wigan), Karl Pratt (Bradford), Gareth Raynor (Hull), Ewan Dowes (Hull), Garreth Carvell (Hull) and Nick Fozzard (St Helens). Carl Ablett was the 100th player to pull on a Rhinos shirt in the competition and he is also the first person alphabetically in the complete list of Super League gladiators.

MOST ARDUOUS CAMPAIGN

The highest number of fixtures played in a season by Leeds was in 1972/3 when they took to the field 52 times. The Loiners played in 34 championship clashes, finishing third, and although knocked out in the first round of the Challenge Cup – at home to Wigan – and second of the Floodlit Trophy – away at Widnes – they reached three other knockout finals. They were comprehensive winners of the Yorkshire Cup, running up 117 points in four ties and thrashing Dewsbury in the final at Odsal 36–9, skipper John Holmes posting a hat-trick. They won the John Player Trophy for the first time, the run including a third round replay against Hull – which took place two days after a drawn game at the Boulevard – and they looked destined to retain the Championship title after sweeping aside Bramley and Castleford and holding on against St Helens in the play-off semi at Headingley. They faced eighth-placed Dewsbury again in the decider, hooker and now Sky Sports pundit Mike Stephenson a hero for the underdogs as Alan Hardisty was dismissed for the first time in his illustrious career. The seasons preceding and post that campaign each contained 51 matches, and the 1970/1 list 50 encounters in an era when part-time, top players really were tested to the physical limit. The only other time Leeds had to play a half century of games was in 1927/8 when stellar Aussies

Jeff Moores and Frank O'Rourke joined the club. They took to the field in league matches 43 times, including twice at York after the first game was abandoned with the home side leading 3–2 when heavy fog rolled in. Clarence Street was also where Yorkshire Cup hopes came to nought in the second round, with interest in the Challenge Cup and play-offs ending at the semi-final stage, to Warrington at Rochdale and home to Featherstone, respectively. Prop and tourist Joe Thompson created a landmark that year when he became the first Leeds player to kick over 100 goals in a season, his last of six successful attempts in the rearranged match at York taking him to 101.

ON NEUTRAL SOIL

Although their home stadium has staged some of the most historic matches in the code's history, when the Rhinos ran out at Old Trafford for their fifth Grand Final in six years, it was the 120th time they had played a competitive game on a neutral ground. That excludes the cricket field at Headingley which was used when the rugby pitch was frozen and unplayable on Christmas Eve, 1938. The neutral-venue matches have taken place in Championship play-offs, Challenge Cup ties, the respective variants of the John Player Trophy, County Cup finals, the Charity Shield, Grand Finals, World Club Challenges and 'on the road' games. In all they have encompassed 25 different places spanning 5 European countries; 8 of them, as has been the trend in recent times, shared soccer grounds. The first occasion Leeds played on neutral soil was on 2 April 1910 when they faced Warrington at Wheater's Field, Manchester, the home of Broughton Rangers. Tries from Walter Goldthorpe, Fred Barron and Fred Webster, together with a goal from Frank Young saw them home 11–10. That sent them through to their first finals because it took a replay – and two matches in three days, both at Huddersfield's Fartown ground – to defeat Hull. Initially, Huddersfield's old home was a happy neutral hunting ground for the Loiners as the first seven times they played there they were undefeated, drawing three and winning four encounters. Huddersfield themselves were Leeds' opponents the first time they played on non-partisan soil in the Championship final five years later, the claret and gold 'team of all talents' handing out a 35–2 thrashing at Belle Vue, Wakefield. In the Yorkshire Cup, Huddersfield were also the initial side to stand in the way in a final, this time staged at Thrum Hall, Halifax, and although the place may have changed, the outcome didn't as they ran out 24–5 victors in November 1919. The ground that Leeds have appeared most at outside of regular league fixtures is Odsal, Bradford, playing host to their silverware quests on 19 occasions with the Loiners winning 11 times, the most famous being their first Championship title success in 1961. Only one match has ended in a 0–0 scoreline, the other encounter at Broughton, against Barrow in a cup semi-final in 1923. That run was the second occasion on which Leeds won the trophy, with the Shipbuilders being beaten 20–0 in the replay on the only time that Leeds have played at Salford, all the points coming in the final 17 minutes.

Leeds Record on Neutral Soil

	P	W	L	D	F	A
Odsal	19	11	7	1	282	236
Fartown	16	8	4	4	168	128
Wembley	11	6	5	0	170	152
Belle Vue	10	6	3	1	105	102
Central Park	9	5	4	0	97	127
Elland Road	9	4	4	1	172	162
Galpharm	7	4	3	0	172	154
Old Trafford	7	4	3	0	113	134

	P	W	L	D	F	A
Thrum Hall	6	3	3	0	29	41
Station Road	5	2	3	0	50	43
Millennium	4	2	2	0	126	111
JJB Stadium	2	0	2	0	38	69
Murrayfield	2	1	1	0	54	40
Broughton	2	1	1	0	11	10
Parkside	1	1	0	0	13	0
Crown Flatt	1	0	0	1	5	5
Salford	1	1	0	0	20	0
Rochdale	1	0	1	0	2	9
Dublin	1	0	1	0	20	45
Boothferry Pk	1	0	1	0	6	18
Burnden Park	1	1	0	0	19	6
Valley Parade	1	1	0	0	22	15
Bootham Cres	1	1	0	0	28	9
Gateshead	1	1	0	0	34	16
Perpignan	1	0	1	0	24	32
TOTALS	120	63	49	8	1780	1664

Leeds were fortunate enough to play five finals at headquarters rather than on a neutral venue, winning them all. Four were in the county cup in the 1970s and early 1980s when sponsors Esso wanted Headingley guaranteed as the home of the decider, irrespective of who was in it. As a result, Leeds beat Wakefield, Hull K.R., Featherstone and Halifax on their way to claiming the Yorkshire crown. Similarly, the only time they have won the BBC2 Floodlit Trophy in 1971, the final was at home with St Helens vanquished 9–5. In those 120 fixtures, Leeds have faced 26 different teams. St Helens have stood in the way of glory the most times, on 14 occasions, although surprisingly the sides did not meet for the first time until 1970, at Odsal in the Championship final. They have a perfect record against four clubs, Whitehaven – who they only faced once – York, Salford and Castleford.

Teams Leeds have met on neutral soil

St Helens – 14 times
Bradford – 11
Wakefield – 11
Huddersfield – 10
Wigan – 9
Warrington – 8
Widnes – 7
Halifax – 6
Hull – 6
Featherstone - 5
Barrow – 4
Hull K.R. – 4
Castleford – 4
Salford – 3
Dewsbury – 3
London – 2
Leigh – 2
York – 2
Swinton – 2
Hunslet – 1
Whitehaven – 1
Catalans – 1
Toulouse – 1
Manly – 1
Canterbury – 1
Melbourne - 1

TOTAL – 120

LEEDS IN THE WILD

A Leeds team made up from the natural world:

Vic Feather
Mick Crane
Russell Robins
Chimpy Busch
Adrian Vowles
W. Woolf
Bill Drake
David Gibbons
Dave Heron
Jamie Peacock
Phil Fox
Mike Ratu
Russ Sowden

NATIONAL STRIP

Boom-winger Ryan Hall became the 52nd Leeds player to be selected for an international side since the advent of Super League. The club have supplied representatives for eight nationalities with Barrie McDermott and Francis Cummins having the distinction of pulling on three different shirts. In the inaugural summer season of 1996, McDermott along with Adrian Morley donned the England strip in the European Championship, Cummins doing likewise two years later when he also won GB honours. Barrie had to wait until 2001 to make his GB bow in the Test arena when he appeared in his first Ashes Series, having worn the emerald of Ireland in the 2000 World Cup. Francis joined him as a Wolfhound the following season and both won their final international caps for the Irish as Rhinos in 2005. The club's first summer internationals were Neil Harmon, who played in four tour games on Great Britain's ill-fated trip to Papua New Guinea, Fiji and New Zealand in 1996, and Morley. The season that saw the most Rhinos capped was 2000, primarily because of the World Cup, which meant 18 players taking the field for 5 different nations. There have been different variants of the England side over the period, England 'A' being used to give aspiring young talent the chance to experience the more rarefied air, which was first brought into being in 2002. Six players went on tour with them to Fiji and Tonga at the end of that season under John Kear's charge; Mark Calderwood, Rob Burrow, Danny Ward, Jamie Jones-Buchanan, Danny McGuire and Matt Diskin. The year before, five Leeds players toured South Africa for the England Under-21s playing two tests against their version of the Rhinos, McGuire scoring a hat-trick in each and Burrow kicking 27 goals in all. The first Super League Academy Tour, to New Zealand in 1996, featured five Leeds players; Marvin Golden, Gavin Brown, Nick Fozzard, Jamie Field and Terry Newton. Both Kevin Sinfield and Lee Smith have scored hat-tricks for England in World Cups, eight years apart, against Russia and Papua New Guinea respectively. Six players – Gareth Hewitt, Scott Rhodes, Hefin O'Hare, Tommy and John Gallagher and Lewis Taylor – have represented their country but not played a first-team Super League game for

Leeds, while Eric Anselme was listed as a Leeds player for France in the 2008 World Cup although his loan spell had effectively ended.

Rhinos Summer Internationals (first appearance in brackets)

Great Britain
Neil Harmon (1996), Adrian Morley (1996), Darren Fleary (1998), Iestyn Harris (1998), Francis Cummins (1998), Terry Newton (1998), Keith Senior (1999), Ryan Sheridan (1999), Kevin Sinfield (1999), Barrie McDermott (2001), Karl Pratt (2002), Gary Connolly (2003), Ryan Bailey (2004), Matt Diskin (2004), Danny McGuire (2004), Danny Ward (2004), Chev Walker (2004), Rob Burrow (2005), Gareth Ellis (2005), Jamie Peacock (2006), Jamie Jones-Buchanan (2007) – Total 21

England
Adrian Morley (1996), Barrie McDermott (1996), Paul Sterling (1998), Francis Cummins (1998), Darren Fleary (1998), Andy Hay (1998), Marcus St Hilaire (1999), Terry Newton (1999), Anthony Farrell (1999), Lee Jackson (1999), Keith Senior (2000), Kevin Sinfield (2000), Chev Walker (2000), Karl Pratt (2001), Rob Burrow (2004), Nick Scruton (2004), Mark Calderwood (2004), Richie Mathers (2005), Jamie Jones-Buchanan (2005), Lee Smith (2006), Ashley Gibson (2006), Danny Williams (2006), Matt Diskin (2006), Ryan Bailey (2006), Gareth Ellis (2008), Jamie Peacock (2008), Ryan Hall (2009) – Total 27

Ireland
Barrie McDermott (1997), Jamie Mathiou (1999), David Barnhill (2000), Ryan Sheridan (2000), Francis Cummins (2001), Tommy Gallagher (2003), John Gallagher (2004) – Total 7

Wales
Iestyn Harris (1998), Paul Sterling (2000), Hefin O'Hare (2000), Anthony Farrell (2000), Garreth Carvell (2000), Lewis Taylor (2004) – Total 6

Scotland
Gareth Hewitt (1998), Scott Rhodes (1999), Graham Mackay (2000), Gareth Morton (2001), Wayne McDonald (2003) – Total 5

New Zealand
Richie Blackmore (2000), Ali Lauitiiti (2004), Willie Poching (2005), Clinton Toopi (2007) – Total 4

Samoa
Ali Lauitiiti (2007), Kylie Leuluai (2008) - Total 2

France
Eric Anselme (2008) - Total 1

As well as current GB and England skipper Jamie Peacock, the period has produced two other international captains from the blue and amber ranks in Barrie McDermott and Iestyn Harris. Not surprisingly, enduring Keith Senior has the longest unbroken run, having appeared in at least one international series every season he has been with the club until his representative retirement in 2008.

SAME NICKNAME 100 YEARS APART

Signed from Tredegar in January 1906, having starred initially for Cardiff, Frank Young was so good under a high ball that he quickly earned the nickname 'bucket' from the Loiners faithful. A master of the kicking game, he appeared 159 times for Leeds and his form was such in 1910 – when he was a vital cog in Leeds' first-ever Northern Union Cup winning team – that he was selected for the inaugural Lions tour. Captured in 2006 from Wests Tigers where he was a Grand Final winner, second-rower Mark O'Neill managed only 11 appearances for the club, 9 off the bench, because of injury. An important influence off the field, he earned the same epithet for the size of his posterior.

THEY SAID IT

'The main ingredient of stardom is the rest of the team.'

Mantra frequently impressed upon his Leeds Academy side by superstar mentor Dean Bell

HOME-GROWN PRODUCTS

Of the 129 players Leeds have used in the Super League up to the end of the 2009 season, including those who were already on contract when the summer switch commenced, just under half have come through the much vaunted Academy structure. A total of 57 graduates have made the first team, some 44 per cent, as opposed to 72 players who have been 'brought in', with 30 of those gladiators having been recruited from abroad. That figure does include former Great Britain hooker Lee Jackson who was signed from Newcastle Knights but not overseas players like, for example, George Mann, Gary Mercer, Adrian Vowles or Andrew Dunemann, who were captured from British clubs. Only one of the 'foreign legion' was snared from Europe, Frenchman Eric Anselme. Former All Black Craig Innes was with the club in 1996 but is not in the total having played only two matches, both of them Challenge Cup ties, before joining Manly in the then divided Australian competition. Six others, including Aussie Graham Mackay, who arrived from French side Beziers, were recruited from rugby union; three of them, Jim Fallon, Alan Tait and Sateki Tuipulotu only appearing fleetingly, in that disastrous inaugural campaign. The most fertile hunting ground has been the New Zealand née Auckland Warriors who have provided seven of their finest exponents for the blue and amber, one of fifteen NRL clubs through which Leeds have trawled their net. Two of them were only in existence for a short time, Graham Murray's Hunter Mariners, where Brad Godden was plying his trade, and South Queensland Crushers, from whom Wayne Collins was acquired. Widnes, Wakefield with the addition of Jay Pitts in 2009 and Sheffield Eagles are the domestic sides raided the most and in all, 16 different clubs in the domestic game have yielded a player to the Rhinos. Four of them – Featherstone, Huddersfield, Hunslet and York – were outside the top flight at the time. In 2010, Leeds are set to unveil four newcomers, Kiwi Test star Greg Eastwood, Australian centre Brett Delaney from Gold Coast Titans, Whitehaven's Kyle Amor and Michael Coady ex-Doncaster.

Signings breakdown

Where Leeds have acquired their players from since the start of Super League:

Academy – 57
Domestic competition – 37
NRL – 26
Rugby union – 6
New Zealand – 2
France – 1

Total – 129

Where they came from

Home	**Abroad**
Sheffield – 5	Auckland/NZ Warriors – 7
Widnes – 5	Northern Eagles/Manly – 3
Wakefield – 5	Melbourne – 2
Keighley – 3	Newcastle – 2
Warrington – 3	North Queensland – 2
Wigan – 3	Brisbane – 1
Bradford – 2	Canberra – 1
Castleford – 2	Canterbury – 1
St Helens – 2	Cronulla – 1
Featherstone – 1	Hunter Mariners – 1
Halifax – 1	Penrith – 1
Huddersfield – 1	South Queensland – 1
Hull – 1	South Sydney – 1
Hunslet – 1	Sydney Roosters – 1
Salford – 1	Wests – 1
York – 1	
Total – 37	Total – 26

Of the six coaches Leeds have had in the fourteen seasons of Super League, three have been Aussies (Graham Murray, Dean Lance, Tony Smith), two proud Kiwis (Dean Bell, Brian McClennan) and one an Englishman (Daryl Powell).

STARS IN THEIR EYES

In 2004, and three weeks before the first grade sides met at Old Trafford, the Senior Academy teams of Leeds and Bradford faced each other in their Grand Final, staged at Headingley Carnegie Stadium as the Rhinos were the Minor Premiers. Scoring four tries to three, and having led 10–6 at the break, the Bulls pulled off a memorable victory. In what was an astonishing crop of talent, 19 of the 34 players on show that night subsequently played Super League although some, admittedly, only briefly. Contrastingly, only three of the nine young Rhinos who did eventually wear the blue and amber, while all but one of the ten Bulls appeared for Bradford, the exception being Leeds-born Ryan Atkins. Nick Scruton has gone on to represent both clubs at the top level with distinction.

Senior Academy Grand Final 2004 – Leeds 18 Bradford 20 – Headingley Carnegie

RHINOS	BULLS
1 Lee Smith (3 goals) ⋆	1 Nicky Saxton (try)
2 Mat Gardner ⋆	2 Paul Clarke
3 Dwayne Barker ⋆	3 Richard Johnson ⋆
4 Chris Buttery	4 Ryan Atkins ⋆
5 Peter Fox ⋆	5 Andy Smith (try) ⋆
6 Tommy Gallagher (try) ⋆	6 Karl Pryce (try, goal) ⋆
7 John Gallagher (2 tries)	7 Richard Colley ⋆
8 Luke Stenchion	17 Matt James ⋆
9 Jon Wainhouse	9 Richard Dobson (goal)
10 Lewis Taylor	10 Jason Boults
11 Jason Golden ⋆	11 Matt Cook ⋆
12 Dave Toothill ⋆	12 Alex Szostak
13 Karl Ablett ⋆	13 Aaron Smith ⋆
Subs (all used)	
14 Dave Doherty	8 Anthony Tonks
15 Aaron Pratt	14 Dave Halley ⋆
16 Nick Scruton ⋆	15 Justin Hunter (try)
17 Matt Carbutt	16 Craig Kopczak ⋆

⋆ – played in Super League

THEY SAID IT

'Never was there a man less likely to have his head turned by fame or flattery. There was something reassuringly solid about that massive figure, that firmly moulded beak of a nose and that determined jutting jaw, its severity relieved by the bald patch which gave him an almost scholarly air.'

Esteemed *Yorkshire Post* journalist Alfred Drewry, eulogising about legendary Leeds forward – and record breaking three-time tourist – Joe Thompson

POINTS MAKE PRIZES

Ever innovative, Rugby League last changed its scoring system before the start of the 1983/4 campaign, increasing the value of a try from 3 points to 4. It thereby maintained the code's historic 'entertainment principle' and further emphasised the priority of handling over kicking. The first Leeds player to score a 4-point try was second-rower Kevin Rayne, from a Roy Dickinson pass, between the posts at Watersheddings in a 25–16 defeat against Oldham. Mick Worrall and Ray Ashton, who were later to become Loiners, crossed the whitewash for the hosts. Immediately, and combined with the new handover rule that further speeded up play, aggregate scores increased with, at the end of the first year, 50 points being posted by a team on 31 occasions as opposed to 11 the year before.

Twice that year Leeds were on the receiving end, at Castleford and Hull K.R. It took the Loiners another four years before they achieved a half century in a league fixture, beating Salford 60–6 at home in September 1987 and they reached that benchmark again on only eight more occasions until the switch to summer. In February 1990, Loiners set a new club top division record with a 90–0 win over Barrow at

Headingley and, memorably, in four days in April 1994 they wracked up 110 points with a 52–20 success at Hilton Park against Leigh, followed by a midweek 58–16 thrashing of Widnes back home. Since the advent of Super League, Leeds have registered over 50 points on more than one occasion in every season except 2000, including even their disastrous 1996 campaign when Workington were humbled 68–28. Having reached the landmark just nine times from 1983 to 1995, they have surpassed it on an astonishing 41 occasions since the switch to summer; the most prolific season being in 2005 when they did it on eight occasions while, ironically, surrendering their title. In 2009, the big wins came on consecutive weeks, the Rhinos racking up 134 points as they hit form for the title run in.

Leeds scoring 50 or more points since the advent of 4 points for a try

1987 – Salford (H) 60–6
1990 – Barrow (H) 90–0
St Helens (H) 50–14
1991 – Rochdale (H) 64–4
Featherstone (A) 52–20
1994 – Leigh (A) 52–20
Widnes (H) 58–16
1995 – Halifax (H) 60–27
Workington (H) 50–12

Total – 9

Leeds scoring 50 or more in Super League

1996 – Workington (H) 68–28
1997 – Warrington (H) 50–12
1998 – Huddersfield (H) 54–4
Huddersfield (A) 72–16

1999 – Halifax (H) 70–22
Castleford (H) 50–22
Huddersfield (H) 86–6
Salford (H) 50–16
2001 – London (A) 50–18
St Helens (H) 74–16
Huddersfield (H) 52–46
Salford (H) 56–6
2002 – Warrington (A) 50–28
Wakefield (H) 52–22
Hull (H) 52–10
2003 – Halifax (H) 54–6
2004 – London (H) 58–14
St Helens (H) 70–0
Castleford (H) 64–12
2005 – Widnes (H) 66–8
Huddersfield (A) 54–10
London (H) 64–6
Leigh (A) 60–4
Wakefield (A) 70–6
Wigan (H) 70–0
Salford (H) 54–14
Leigh (A) 74–0
2006 – Castleford (H) 66–14
Catalans (A) 58–10
Harlequins (A) 60–0
Warrington (H) 54–16
Catalans (H) 60–12
2007 – Warrington (A) 52–10
Catalans (H) 54–8
Harlequins (A) 54–20
Salford (H) 52–14
2008 – Wakefield (H) 58–12
Castleford (H) 54–12
Wigan (A) 52–16

2009 – Castleford (H) 76–12
Celtic (A) 68–0

Total – 41

WHICH WAY LEEDS

A blue and amber squad which should have a good sense of place:

Graham Middleton
W. Rhodes
Mark Calderwood
Jeff Townend
Graham Eccles
W. Westmoreland
Dennis Scholes
Joe Brittain
Adrian Morley
Harry Street
Gareth Morton
J. Windsor
Willie Oulton
E. Woolley
S. Burnley
Charlie Glossop
H. Blackburn

SQUAD SIZE

If the ideal number of players in a Super League squad (under the restrictions of the salary cap) is 25, Leeds have only used that number, or less, in four Super League seasons. In 1998 and 2007, both years they reached Old Trafford, success was built on the back of only 23 bodies. The only other seasons to hit the mark were 2003 and 2005. The greatest turnover of players was in the *annus horribilis* of 1996, when the club begged and borrowed to maintain their top flight status, using 39 participants including coach Dean Bell. Some have pointed to avoiding injuries being a crucial factor in winning the competition but the total of 31 players used in 2008, as the crown was retained, was their highest for eight seasons.

Number of players used by the Rhinos in a summer season

1996 – 39
1997 – 32
1998 – 23
1999 – 30
2000 – 29
2001 – 30
2002 – 28
2003 – 24
2004 – 26
2005 – 25
2006 – 27
2007 – 23
2008 – 31
2009 – 27

THEY SAID IT

'I was pretty close to Derek Noonan at the end when he dropped the ball and I'm convinced he wouldn't have scored anyway. There were about five of us covering across and, if he'd caught it, we would have taken him out.'

Loiners centre Les Dyl on the dramatic climax to the epic 1978 cup final against Saints.

HELPING HAND

Leeds have allowed eleven players to go out on loan to other Super League sides over the last ten seasons. The first to take up temporary residence was Garreth Carvell, who made eight appearances for Gateshead in their only campaign in the top flight in 1999, scoring his sole try in a win at Huddersfield. His form for Thunder was such that when the club merged with Hull and Shaun McRae moved over to take up the reins there, he came back for the rampaging former Stanningley junior on a permanent basis. To the black and whites is where three of the other loanees have gone, the most recent being young winger Jodie Broughton who was re-engaged in 2009 after impressing in a five-match spell there in 2008. Nick Scruton made 18 appearances at the KC Stadium in 2004, all but two off the bench, while Danny Williams played three games for them four seasons later. The side who have taken advantage of the Rhinos' largesse the most is London Broncos/Harlequins RL, including the most notorious switch, which came back to haunt the generosity of the Headingley Carnegie management and coaching staff. That was in 2004 when back-rower Liam Botham, son of Ian, in his penultimate of eight matches in the capital, showed his parent club exactly what they were missing. Having already scored a try and three goals in a storming display, he stepped up to convert Lee Greenwood's last-minute touchdown out wide to salvage a point in a 36–36 draw against Tony Smith's champions-elect. Others to serve apprenticeships in the smoke were Jon Hepworth (2002 – 2 appearances), Scott Murrell (2004 – 6 appearances) and Luke Burgess (2007 – 3 appearances). Further loanees have been Chris Feather who had two stints back at his old club Wakefield in 2004 and again the following year, Richie Mathers who had a short spell with his current club Warrington in 2002 and perhaps the most surprising of all, Jordan Tansey's secondment to Sydney Roosters at the end of the 2008 season. That was initially for two years although he was brought back early by Hull, debuting for them in late 2009. Mike Ratu was sent out on loan but that was to Championship side Halifax in 2008. In 2010, which will see the advent of dual registrations, Simon Worrall (Toulouse), Ben Jones-Bishop (Harlequins), Kyle Amor (Whitehaven), Michael Coady (Featherstone) and Dane Manning (Featherstone), are all set to gain valuable experience elsewhere.

Indicating the wealth of talent that has been nurtured by the club in recent seasons, an entire side by position can be selected of ex-Leeds players, all but one still at the top level in 2009. Amazingly, fourteen of them have come through the vaunted Rhinos Academy system. Added to this mythical selection, wingers Peter Fox and Mike Wainwright are currently starring with Hull K.R. and Castleford respectively but did not make a first team appearance for Leeds while Danny Williams and Clinton Toopi are plying their trade in rugby union.

Super League XIV Old Boys XVII

1 Richie Mathers (Warrington)
2 Mark Calderwood (Hull)
3 Chev Walker (Hull K.R.)
4 Tonie Carroll (Brisbane Broncos)
5 Gareth Raynor (Hull)
6 Iestyn Harris (retired 2009 at Featherstone)
7 Jordan Tansey (Hull)
8 Garreth Carvell (Warrington)
9 Terry Newton (Bradford – 2010 Wakefield)
10 Nick Fozzard (Hull K.R. – 2010 St Helens)
11 Adrian Morley (Warrington)
12 Nick Scruton (Bradford)
13 Scott Murrell (Hull K.R.)

Subs
14 Ben Kaye (Harlequins)
15 Danny Ward (Harlequins)
16 Jason Netherton (Hull K.R.)
17 Jamie Thackray (Hull)

GOLDEN TRIES & GOALS

Only 20 players in the 119-year history of the club have scored in a Championship or Grand Final. In fact, a Leeds player crossing the whitewash in the ultimate decider was incredibly rare until their first victory in 1961. Including a replay – in 1930 – the club appeared in six finals prior to that inaugural success but only touched down once, former Otley RU winger Les Grainge finding the line in the 1931 defeat by Swinton. With his two scores at Old Trafford in 2008, Danny McGuire became the leading poacher of golden tries for the club, taking his tally to four and becoming the first player to score in three different last-night clashes in the Super League era, feats matched by Lee Smith in 2009. John Atkinson and Ronnie Cowan scored a try in two different finals and Derek Hallas grabbed a brace in that emotional 1961 triumph. Kevin Sinfield's three successes in 2009 – two conversions and a drop goal – extended his lead for goals in the title clincher. Behind him comes Lewis Jones who knocked over five – the highest Leeds total in such a game; Terry Clawson with four, including three when picking up the Harry Sunderland Trophy in 1972, a total he shares with Bev Risman and John Holmes while Joe Thompson claimed three. In total, eleven players have scored points with the boot on the 16 occasions the blue and amber have contested the big prize, Bill Ramsey's and Rob Burrow's being drop goals.

CLOSEST CAMPAIGNS

Much has rightly been made about the increasing incidence of uncertainty of outcome during the Super League XIV campaign. Kevin Sinfield's extraordinarily dramatic, at-the-death, match-winning conversion to deny Warrington was the sixth time in 2009 that the Rhinos had triumphed by 6 points or less and secured a double, in that manner, over the Wolves. They made it seven in clinching the League Leader's Shield at Salford in the final regular season round. On four of those occasions the decisive margin has been 2 points but, including the play-offs, the maximum number of close games in a year – using the one converted score criterion – is 9, which has actually been the case in 6 of the previous 13 seasons. The Rhinos were at their most dominant when winning the title in 2004 and again in the early stages of the following campaign when they were in irresistible form, but the competition has involved approximately a third of their fixtures being deemed 'close' in six out of the last ten seasons. The highest number of narrow wins and defeats came in 2006, when seven of the nine one-score games were determined by no more than a goal; including defeats in the first round of the play-offs at home to Warrington and away at Cas in the regular season where the difference was a drop goal, as it was when Salford were on the receiving end at Headingley Carnegie. Defeat at home in the 2003 Final Eliminator was also by an agonising point and one Grand Final falls into the one-score category, the inaugural one in 1998, when Wigan beat Leeds 10–4. Although narrow margin contests were less prevalent in the earlier years of Super League, battles with Sheffield were always closely fought affairs. Keith Senior was a try-scorer for the Eagles when they won 34–31 at Bramall Lane in 1996 after Leeds had battled back from 16–0 down. The following year, at home, Leeds led 22–14 with 3 minutes to go but a last-gasp Mark Aston conversion from the touchline took the points. In

1998 it was the Rhinos' turn at the Don Valley Stadium when they staged an astonishing recovery to win the match with the last kick. The one-score sequence was extended the next year when Sheffield won 22–16 at home, Aussie Jeff Hardy scoring the winning try 4 minutes from time after Graham Murray's men had led by 10 points at the break.

LONGEST TIME BETWEEN DRINKS

Jim Brough, one of the most cultured full-backs to play for the club, and John Atkinson, the classiest of finishers, share a distinction of winning Challenge Cup medals ten years apart. Cumbrian maestro Brough led the rearguard action as Barrow were beaten in the 'final that Wembley forgot' in 1932 at Central Park, returning as skipper and at 39 years old, as the side took the wartime spoils in 1942 against Halifax. The deadly Atkinson was granted possibly the most controversial try ever at the Twin Towers in the 'watersplash' victory of 1968 and started the revival against St Helens in the 'comeback' final ten seasons later. Two players have appeared in Challenge Cup finals nine years apart; Joe Thompson a winner and ace marksman in both 1923 – barely three months after he signed – and again in 1932, landing nine goals in all, and Francis Cummins, who was a loser as the youngest ever to grace the Twin Towers in 1994 and again against Bradford, in Cardiff, in 2003.

TOP OF THE CHARTS

England winger Ryan Hall ended his first full season in 2009 as leading try-scorer, finishing 11 ahead of his nearest rival, almost a third more. His season total of 34 included one try on his international debut in Paris and a further score in the Four Nations Tournament – a length-of-the-field interception – also against the French. He became the first player in blue and amber to be the leading poacher in all competitions since Mark Calderwood in 2005 although, unlike Hall, he was not the top scorer in the Super League season that year including play-offs. Before that, another winger, John Atkinson, achieved the feat in 1972/3 when he grabbed 39 touchdowns. That was the third time in four seasons 'Atky' had been the code's most productive. The year he missed out, Leeds' Bob Haigh set a world record of 40 touchdowns for a forward (later beaten by Ellery Hanley in his third season at Headingley in 1994/5), a total he shared with St Helens winger Les Jones. Atkinson too was a joint-top scorer in 1971/2 with Bradford winger Mike Lamb, who was a PE teacher at Leeds Grammar School and had come through the junior ranks at Headingley before being released to make his name at Odsal, going on to play for Bradford at Wembley. Only two other Leeds players have topped the try charts. The inimitable Eric Harris did so five times in his eight seasons from 1930–8 including twice breaking the club tries in a season total with 58 in his debut year and 63 in 1935/6, which included one at Wembley. The other top poacher was Welshman W. Evans who was signed from Leeds Parish Church when they disbanded and crossed 27 times in 1902/3. Twice in the Super League era Leeds players have finished joint top 4-point kings but were deemed to be runners-up by virtue of the touchdowns they posted in the play-offs. In 2004, Danny McGuire and Lesley Vainikolo both found the whitewash 38 times, McGuire's last of the season the winner in the Grand Final against his rival's men, while in 2007 Brent Webb shared the honour with Paul Wellens with 24, again the Leeds custodian scoring the last of his post-season efforts at Old Trafford, against his challengers side.

THEY SAID IT

'My only regret is that I didn't do myself justice in my time at Leeds. It was an ideal opportunity to enhance myself and I should have used it as a platform for a long and successful international career. I'm just sorry that I didn't take it and that the Leeds fans never saw the best of me.'

Prop Lee Crooks on his eventual retirement

'I had a dream last night I was going to get a hat-trick so I'm gutted! I don't score many tries but to do it in a Grand Final on such an occasion is unbelievable, absolutely brilliant.'

Rhinos hooker and Harry Sunderland winner Matt Diskin reflects on his 2004 Old Trafford score that helped bring the title back to Headingley Carnegie after 32 years

GIVE US A JOB

A Leeds team of the era who whose names hint at alternative occupations:

Dennis Warrior
Billy Banks
Steve Pilgrim
Mark Lord
Tony Fisher
T. Taylor
G. Shepherd
C. Law
Sean Miller
Kevin Squire
Colin Cooper
Fred Barron
Dean Clark
Paul Cook
Harry Dyer
Des Foreman
Andy Mason

SHARING THE LOAD

One of the indicators of a shared workload is the number of players in a team who reach double figures in the try-scoring stakes in a season. Keith Senior's brace and Jamie Jones-Buchanan's surging effort against Celtic Crusaders in Newport, followed by a double for Lee Smith in the play-off at home to Hull K.R., meant that seven of the squad reached the benchmark in 2009. The average number of Rhinos to hit that target in a Super League season is six, although that is lessened somewhat by the opening three campaigns. They yielded a total of only ten occasions when the whitewash was crossed ten times or more.

The greatest number of double-figure achievers in any given campaign was ten in 2005 when the Rhinos were desperately close to pulling-off a domestic double but had to settle for success in the World Club Challenge. Surprisingly, perhaps, only four players registered the feat when the Super League title was regained in 2007 – Brent Webb, Danny McGuire, Rob Burrow and Scott Donald – who between them accounted for exactly half of the tries scored that year, 77 out of 154. Backs, inevitably, take the glory but the greatest number of tries in a summer season scored by a pack star is 14 by Ali Lauitiiti in 2005, aided by his astonishing five off the bench at Wakefield. The panic-inducing Samoan was also the leading scoring forward for the club in 2008 with 11 touchdowns. Assistant coach Willie Poching is the most prolific from within the scrum on a seasonal basis, heading the list on three occasions between 2003 and 2006, although only in the first of those years did he claim the honour outright. Adrian Morley, Kevin Sinfield – seven years apart – and Andy Hay have all had that honour twice.

Rhinos' leading forward try-scorer in Super League

1996 – 7 tries, Gary Mercer, Mick Shaw
1997 – 9 tries, Anthony Farrell, Barrie McDermott
1998 – 9 tries, Adrian Morley
1999 – 11 tries, Andy Hay
2000 – 8 tries, Adrian Morley
2001 – 10 tries, Kevin Sinfield
2002 – 11 tries, Andy Hay
2003 – 12 tries, Willie Poching
2004 – 12 tries, Willie Poching, Matt Diskin
2005 – 14 tries, Ali Lauitiiti
2006 – 8 tries, Gareth Ellis, Willie Poching
2007 – 6 tries, Kevin Sinfield
2008 – 11 tries, Ali Lauitiiti
2009 – 10 tries, Jamie Jones-Buchanan

ON THE POINT OF HISTORY

Never in the top flight have Leeds had the leading try-scorer, goal-kicker and points-gatherer in the same campaign, although they did come agonisingly close in 2009. Ryan Hall topped the try charts and Kevin Sinfield the goals with 136 including three drop goals, which included his historic 1,000th successful kick in the colours at Celtic. With five tries, his points tally amounted to 289, just 11 short of Wigan and Ireland's Pat Richards. In 2004 Leeds came closest to the clean sweep, Danny McGuire finishing level with Lesley Vainikolo for tries but being placed below him having scored one less in the regular rounds, while skipper Sinfield headed the goals and points on his way to lifting the Super League trophy. In 2007, when Sinfield again claimed the goals scored and points tally honours on his way to becoming the first Leeds player to play and score in every game in a season, Henry Fa'afili was deemed the top try-scorer by virtue of his regular season record being one better than Brent Webb's. Skipper supreme Sinfield was the top goal-kicker again in 2008. Joe Thompson twice, Bert Cook, Lewis Jones and Bev Risman three times in four years are the only other Leeds players to head the goal-kicking charts. When Thompson ruled, Alf Ellaby of St Helens was the top try-scorer and every season Eric Harris headed the try charts during the 1930s, when Thompson was the Leeds marksman, Jim Sullivan of Wigan was the leading goal-kicker. In 1950/1, when Cook's size four ruled, Brian Bevan crossed the whitewash the most times and although Risman's metronomic boot coincided with one of the greatest eras of Leeds back stars, his accuracy never quite coincided with their strike power. All three kickers were leading point-scorers in the seasons they excelled with the boot, except in 1966/7, when Risman headed the goals but St Helens winger Len Killeen the points tally. Lewis Jones's legendary season in 1956/7, which yielded him a world record seasonal points harvest of 496 – encompassing 194 goals – had Wigan's Billy Boston atop the finishers.

PLACE OF WORK

These days the on-field heroes are full-time professionals, dedicated to maximising their performance, with predominantly Kirkstall's training facility their place of work. When Leeds won the title forty years ago in 1969, the players had to take time off from their real jobs to prepare to wrest the ultimate crown from Castleford. Their trades, many of which now seem as foreign as the concept, are listed below as indication of how times have changed.

1 Bev Risman – Schoolmaster
2 Ronnie Cowan – Clothing Worker
3 Syd Hynes – Welder
4 Bernard Watson – Plater
5 John Atkinson – Telegraph Technician
6 Mick Shoebottom – Welder
7 Barry Seabourne – Driver
8 Mick Clark – Sales Rep
9 Tony Crosby – Lift Engineer
10 Ken Eyre – Metal Worker
11 Mick Joyce – Building Worker
12 Bill Ramsey – Casemaker
13 Ray Batten – Stone Mason

Substitutes
14 John Langley – Railway Worker
15 David Hick – Blacksmith

TOP OF THE TREE

The Rhinos' garnering of the League Leader's Shield at the Willows in the final regular season round of the 2009 competition was the eighth time that the club have finished at the head of the standings come the end of the weekly rounds. It took until Lewis Jones' side of 1960/1 to first scale such lofty heights, although there was no formal accolade to commemorate the feat. In 1964/5 – on the reintroduction of a single division of 30 teams – the clubs called for greater recognition of the side finishing top going into, what was then, a top-16 play-off. For nine seasons, until the two division format was tried again, a League Leader's Trophy was instituted. Four clubs had the distinction of displaying it in their cabinets but Leeds monopolised the silverware, bringing it to Headingley on five occasions; St Helens in the first two seasons, Wigan and Warrington the other holders. Leeds first won it in 1966/7 – when the play-offs were restricted to the top four as a one-off – retained it three more times and won it back from Wigan in 1971/2. The greatest number of points Leeds have gathered in a league season is 60, on three occasions. The first, in that historic 1960/1 campaign, came from 36 fixtures, with the other two after 34 encounters. The Loiners' best return was in 1968/9 when they won 29, drew 2 (away at Wakefield and Hull) and lost 3 matches (away to Leigh on the opening day of the season, at St Helens and when visiting Bradford on the last day of the league fixtures). The biggest margin between the blue and amber and their nearest rivals is 9 points, achieved in 1969/70 and again in 2004. Prior to Super League, a different side were runners-up each time behind the triumphant Loiners. Leeds have gone on to lift the title on five occasions after finishing top; in 1960/1, 1968/9, 1971/2, 2004 and 2009. They were denied by Castleford in the second round of the play-offs in 1966/7, Wigan at the same stage the following season and Saints in the Championship final in 1969/70.

When Leeds topped the table

1960/1 – total 60 points ahead by 5 – runners-up Warrington
1966/7 – total 58 points ahead by 4 – runners-up Hull K.R.
1967/8 – total 56 points ahead by 7 – runners-up Wakefield Trinity
1968/9 – total 60 points ahead by 4 – runners-up St Helens
1969/70 – total 60 points ahead by 9 – runners-up Castleford
1971/2 – total 58 points ahead by 4 – runners-up Bradford Northern
2004 – total 50 points ahead by 9 – runners-up Bradford Bulls
2009 – total 42 points ahead by 4 – runners-up St Helens

The only other time Leeds finished ahead of the pile was when they were excluded from the 'Super League' of the time, the newly formed Northern Rugby League in 1901/2 and played in the Yorkshire Senior Competition. Picking up players from the disbanded Leeds Parish Church to bolster their squad, they headed the table by 9 points from Manningham, securing 'promotion'.

THEY SAID IT

'I never saw him do the dirty. We shall miss a player and a gentleman and the greatest football favourite who ever stepped on to the Headingley ground.'

Leeds forward Bernard Gould pays tribute to Australian legend John 'Dinny' Campbell as he prepared to return home to Sydney – where he scouted for and represented the club – in September 1921

TOP FIVE WHO DIDN'T SIGN

Leeds' history is littered with tales – many of them apocryphal – of players whom the club chose not to sign but went on to become world-beaters or whose contracts were supposedly signed and sealed but never actually delivered. Five of the very best who failed to pull on the famous shirt are:

1) BRIAN BEVAN – Deemed by the Headingley hierarchy to be too frail for the big time when recommended to them by Bill Shankland; went on to become the sport's most prolific ever try-scorer at Warrington.

2) KEVIN WARD – Thought to be too small for a forward and too slow to be a centre; became one of the most feared props in both hemispheres with Castleford and Manly.

3) PETER STERLING – Captured the heart of a Leeds girl and was supposedly on his way twice, before and after a cameo stint with Hull, only for injuries to intervene. He did wear blue and amber – but only for his beloved Parramatta.

4) MARK GRAHAM – The Kiwi colossus and inspiring, two-Tour leader was constantly linked with Leeds in the early 1980s but could not be prised from North Sydney; though he eventually had a cameo stint with Wakefield late in his career.

5) TAWERA NIKAU – After making an early impression with York and Sheffield, the New Zealander's contract was apparently secure in the Headingley safe. Castleford – where he is a Hall of Famer – and then Warrington, after a Grand Final win with Melbourne, were his only top flight English clubs as it turned out.

Coach of any 'non-team' would have to be either Frank Stanton or Don Furner who, although frequent advisors to the Leeds Board, could not be tempted to take up the reins at Headingley, despite numerous offers. In the end, Don's son David wore the colours 52 times, his last, glorious appearance being in the 2004 Grand Final when he became one of the few players to pick up a ring in the English and Australian Grand Finals, ten years apart, despite being injured in the Old Trafford warm up.

MADE OF STEEL

Despite their recent successes, it is 11 years since the Rhinos last had a 'Man of Steel' chosen from within their midst. Iestyn Harris – who headed the points list with 283 from 11 tries and 117 goals in 1998 – picked up the highest individual award, sponsored for the first time by JJB Sports, as the club made it to the inaugural Grand Final. It was one of three gongs he was presented with at the end of a majestic season, his first as Leeds skipper, the others being the Player's Player of the Year – ahead of team-mate Adrian Morley – and the Rugby League Writers' Award. The Wales and Great Britain international was the unanimous choice of the panel of selected journalists as the Man of Steel and received a cheque for £5,000 along with the vaunted trophy. The current Welsh coach was the signing that signalled the resurgence of the Rhinos under new owners Paul Caddick and Gary Hetherington when he arrived in 1997 and he still holds three kicking records for the club. Among his just over 1,000 career goals – 601 of which were with Leeds – he landed 17 in a Challenge Cup fourth round tie at Swinton in February 2001, at the start of his final year at the club. His seasonal tally of 168 goals, achieved in 1999, has yet to be surpassed as has his mark for the most successful shots at goal in a Challenge Cup final, which was 8 at the old Wembley against London Broncos during that season. Harris became the third Leeds player to pick up the top individual accolade. The Man of Steel Award was inaugurated in 1977 by the Trumann's Steel Co. of Manchester, Leeds and Liverpool, hence the name, and was instituted not to reward those in the image of their product but 'the personality adjudged to have made the most impact on the season.' Five categories were set up initially, the Division One Player of the Year, his Division Two counterpart, the Young Player of the Year, Coach of the Year and Referee of the Year. That season, a prestigious evening in front of an audience of over 800 at the Golden Garter Theatre Restaurant in Wythenshawe saw the quintet of recipients pick up a cheque for £100 and a set of stainless steel goblets and tray worth £80. One of them was then selected as the ultimate Man of Steel which brought with it a further £250. After cabaret featuring The Barron Knights, Leeds hooker David Ward – on the back of a sensational season that saw him take over the captaincy of the side, gain winners' medals in the Yorkshire Cup and Challenge

Cup, make his debut for Yorkshire, GB U-24s and England, before being selected to tour Down Under as the number one hooker – was chosen as the Young Player of the Year, ahead of Saints' Harry Pinner and Jimmy Crampton from Hull. He then beat off competition from the likes of Malcolm Reilly, voted the First Division's best and St Helens coach Eric Ashton for the big prize. By the time Leeds next had a recipient, in 1991, the format had changed in that the Man of Steel did not have to have won any of the other categories as a pre-requisite and Stones had taken over the sponsorship from Greenall Whitley. Stand-off Garry Schofield received a £4,000 cheque and a £300 silver champagne goblet at the end of a season that had seen him also selected as the Loiners' Player of the Year by a record margin. That added to being Great Britain's best, which brought with it the Ernest Ward Trophy after he had starred in all ten Test matches played that season. Others who have played for Leeds but picked up the Man of Steel while at other clubs are; Ellery Hanley (Wigan – who won it three times in five seasons), Dean Bell (Wigan), James Lowes (Bradford), Adrian Vowles (Castleford) and Jamie Peacock (Bradford) while former coach Doug Laughton was the third player to lift it.

PLAY-OFF KINGS

With Bradford failing to make the post season in the cruellest of circumstances in the last round of the 2009 regular campaign, only Leeds and St Helens have qualified for the Grand Final play-offs every year since they were instituted in 1998. The lowest position the Rhinos have finished in is fifth in 2001, although by virtue of being beaten at home in the elimination game by Warrington in 2006, despite finishing third, they were also ranked fifth once the play-offs had been included. Saints ended the regular campaign in fifth in 2004, their lowest finish, but were ranked sixth following the elimination games, when they lost at Wigan and Wakefield won at Hull. Between them the fiercest of modern day rivals have won 8 of the 12 available titles going.

COACHES PICK

For ten seasons from 1988 until its last publication covering the 1998 campaign the code's bible, the *Rothman's Rugby League Yearbook*, complied by official statisticians Ray Fletcher and David Howes, asked the coaches of the elite clubs to choose their team of the year in a forerunner of the Super League 'Dream Team'. In all, 73 players gained mythical selection, with 7 of them coming from Leeds. They were Francis Cummins, Brad Godden, Ellery Hanley, Iestyn Harris, Adrian Morley, Garry Schofield and Alan Tait. The latter, who was the first Loiner included – in 1992/3 – and was twice selected while with Widnes before that, made the composite team of the decade along with Morley and Hanley. Morley received the coaches' pick three times, from 1996 to 1998, the most for a Headingley representative.

WAR OF THE ROSES

Headingley has staged four County Championship clashes, three against arch rivals Lancashire, all of which were lost. The most bizarre clash was the final one, in June 2002 when Rhinos scrum-half Ryan Sheridan skippered the White Rose county. In an astonishing game of two halves, Lancashire – with Oldhamers Kevin Sinfield and Barrie McDermott in their ranks – led 30–0 at half time. Yorkshire, whose tries all came from Leeds men, Matt Diskin and Karl Pratt with two each and Keith Senior, hit back but went down 38–26. Senior had also scored the year before when Yorkshire lost 36–24. The only victory for the home county came against Cumberland in January 1973, in a play-off after the three counties had won a game each. Les Dyl and Ray Batten were in the side that triumphed 20–7.

THEY SAID IT

'I have followed the team through thick and thin, but we have had more thin than thick. I trust there will now be better things in store for the Leeds club.'

Long time Leeds supporter Richard Scott, speaking at the celebratory dinner in the Headingley Pavilion to commemorate Leeds' first trophy – the winning of the Yorkshire Senior Competition Shield in 1901/2

STRANGE DAYS INDEED

Super League X was an odd season for the Rhinos. Defending champions, they became the best club in the world when defeating Canterbury Bulldogs at a packed Elland Road to open the 2005 campaign. Their form was imperious for the opening half of the season, Easter home defeat to Wakefield their only setback as they piled up the points, becoming the great entertainers. They topped the 70-point barrier 4 times during the summer; against Pia (70–0 at home) in the Challenge Cup, memorably on consecutive weekends at Wakefield (70–6) and hosting Wigan (70–0) while defeating Leigh 74–0 at Hilton Park, Ashley Gibson having an astonishing debut. By the end of the season they had smashed their previous bests for points scored in a league season (1,152 at an average of 41 over 28 rounds) and points in all games (1,424 at an average of 40 from 36 encounters). Despite the flair and panache, Leeds came up domestically empty-handed, losing the League Leader's Shield to St Helens by 3 points, the Challenge Cup final to outsiders Hull by the odd point in 49 and the Grand Final to arch rivals Bradford, 15–6 having taken the quickest route to Old Trafford.

TOP PERFORMERS

Twelve Leeds players have won the top individual award in the two major competitions, Kevin Sinfield the only one to claim both accolades.

Harry Sunderland Trophy (for man of the match in the Championship final/Premiership final/Grand Final)

1968/9 – Bev Risman (full-back v Castleford, at Bradford, won 16–14)
1971/2 – Terry Clawson (prop v St Helens, at Swinton, won 9–5)
1974/5 – Mel Mason (stand-off v St Helens, at Wigan, won 26–11)
1978/9 – Kevin Dick (stand-off v Bradford, at Huddersfield, won 24–2)
2004 – Matt Diskin (hooker v Bradford, at Old Trafford, won 16–8)
2007 – Rob Burrow (scrum-half v St Helens, at Old Trafford, won 33–6)
2008 – Lee Smith (full-back v St Helens, at Old Trafford, won 24–16)

2009 – Kevin Sinfield (loose forward v St Helens, at Old Trafford, won 18–10)

Lance Todd Trophy (for man of the match in the Challenge Cup final)

1957 – Jeff Stevenson (scrum-half v Barrow, at Wembley, won 9–7)
1977 – Steve Pitchford (prop v Widnes, at Wembley, won 16–7)
1999 – Leroy Rivett (winger v London, at Wembley, won 52–16)
2003 – Gary Connolly (full-back v Bradford, at Cardiff, lost, 22–20)
2005 – Kevin Sinfield (stand-off v Bradford, at Cardiff, lost 25–24)

THE LAST WORD

'The biggest thing for me is winning with this bunch of lads, you spend more time with them than anybody and they are a fantastic, honest, hardworking set of guys and when you put so much in you get your rewards. What it takes to win, this team's got it.'

Danny McGuire's dressing room reaction to the Rhinos' 'Three-peat' Grand Final success in 2009